THE GREAT RAILROAD STRIKE IN OHIO

THE GREAT RAILROAD STRIKE IN OHIO

MARK STRECKER

Published by The History Press
An imprint of Arcadia Publishing
Charleston, SC
www.historypress.com

Copyright © 2026 by Mark Strecker
All rights reserved

First published 2026

Manufactured in the United States

ISBN 9781467170857
Hardcover ISBN 9781540299741

Library of Congress Control Number: 2025944851

Notice: The information in this book is true and complete to the best of our knowledge. It is offered without guarantee on the part of the author or The History Press. The author and The History Press disclaim all liability in connection with the use of this book.

All rights reserved. No part of this book may be reproduced or transmitted in any form whatsoever without prior written permission from the publisher except in the case of brief quotations embodied in critical articles and reviews.

CONTENTS

Introduction 7

1. The Panic of 1873 9
2. A Plague of Tramps 23
3. Working on the Railroad 35
4. The Strike Begins 47
5. Railroaded by Standard Oil 57
6. Strike on the Pennsylvania Railroad 67
7. The Strike Spreads to Ohio 77
8. Authority Strikes Back 89
9. The Aftermath 101

Acknowledgements 109
Bibliography 111
Index 117
About the Author 127

INTRODUCTION

Railroads have been so romanticized, it's easy to forget just how awful conditions were for the people who worked for them. It was an extremely dangerous job, especially for the brakemen, who stopped trains by leaping across the tops of cars to apply their handbrakes. Brakemen were also responsible for coupling and uncoupling cars, and few quit or retired with all their fingers. Even the passengers faced peril every time they boarded a train. They risked the far too frequent occurrence of derailments, head-on collisions, or bridges collapsing beneath them. Bystanders minding their own business were often killed by oncoming trains, especially in cities where railroad safety didn't exist. Livestock weren't safe, either. The cowcatcher was meant to push obstacles off the tracks, and living things rarely survived.

The attitude of those who ran the railroads was that laborers were disposable. Improved safety was deemed too costly for implementation, and those who worked for a railroad were hired with the understanding that getting killed or maimed was their problem, not their employer's. At this time, too, most Americans believed that government had no business getting involved in the affairs of business—that was communism! The American elite, in contrast, expected the courts and local law enforcement to do their will, and for the most part, that's what happened. Banks and landlords, after all, needed muscle to deal with delinquents, and courts nearly always sided with businesses over their employees.

When a terrible depression that began with the Panic of 1873 gripped the United States, calls for help from the federal government were condemned by the majority of newspapers. Thousands of unemployed laborers began roaming across America looking for work. They were called "tramps," with all the negative connotations that go with that label. Instead of giving aid, state and local governments criminalized them with vagrancy laws, justifying this by claiming tramps could find work if they really wanted despite the fact none was to be had.

Most charities of the day had the sole goal of bringing religious salvation to the poor, not giving them any meaningful aid. Charities were usually run by the same people who controlled the courts, businesses, and government, and these benefactors rarely met with—let alone got to know—those they purported to help. People who did receive what pittance charities doled out had to be "deserving"—a vague enough designation that most were excluded.

After the Civil War, the United States experienced a massive boom of railroad construction, so much so that by 1877, railroads were the nation's largest employer. Railroads produced staggering profits, nearly all of which went to the stockholders. During the depression of the 1870s, train crews were hit especially hard. Paid by the run, the number of days they worked dropped to three or four a week. To make matters worse, crewmen's wages were cut, repeatedly on some roads. When it became too much and they went on strike, the heads of two of the biggest railroads, the Baltimore & Ohio and the Pennsylvania, called on local politicians to use police to deal with them. When that didn't work, they escalated it to the governors, demanding that they send out their state militias. Many of those in the militias sympathized with the strikers, so the next step was to demand that President Rutherford B. Hayes use the U.S. Army to crush the strike with force.

Ohio followed this pattern to a point, but its response to the strikes was markedly different than neighboring West Virginia and Pennsylvania. This book's focus is on Ohio's experience with the Great Railroad Strike of 1877, which was more accurately a series of separate strikes with roughly the same goals that expanded into other industries. Although the strike didn't begin in Ohio, nor did the Panic of 1873, many of the key players in both events were born or lived in Ohio.

CHAPTER 1

THE PANIC OF 1873

September 15, 1873, wasn't a good day for Jay Cooke, though it started out well enough. President Ulysses S. Grant had stayed overnight at Cooke's Philadelphia house, and the two ate breakfast together. Afterward, Grant headed out west and Cooke went to his office at Jay Cooke & Co., the investment bank he'd cofounded in 1861. On this day, the bank hit its breaking point. At eleven o'clock that morning, Cooke ordered the closure of the Philadelphia branch, this not long after the shuttering of its New York City one. A stoic man not known for showing great emotion, Cooke wept. The bank soon went into receivership.

Upon hearing the news of the firm's collapse, traders in New York City panicked and immediately began selling the rest of the day. Even shares for successful businesses fell. *The Nation* magazine described it like this:

> *If a Roman or a man of the Middle Ages had been suddenly brought into view of the scene, he would have concluded without hesitation that a ruthless invader was coming down the island; that his advanced guard was momentarily expected; and that anybody found by his forces in possession of Western Union, or* [New York &] *Harlem* [Railroad], *or Lake Shore* [& Southern Michigan Railroad], *or any other paying stock or bond, would be subjected to cruel tortures, if not put to death.*

The collapse sparked a financial panic that signaled the beginning of a severe economic depression lasting until 1879.

Cooke was a native of Sandusky, Ohio. His father, Eleutheros, was born in 1787 near the Vermont border in Granville, New York. A lawyer by profession, he married Martha Caswell in 1812 and in 1816 moved her and his young daughter to Madison, Indiana. In 1817, he needed to return to New York for business. To reach it, he traveled overland to Lake Erie, where he took a boat to his final destination. During his trek through Ohio, he met an old friend, Charles Drake, who took him to the burgeoning settlement of Venice, which was southwest of modern Sandusky along Cold Creek. Here the landowner selling lots, Frederic Falley, paid Eleutheros to write up legally binding contracts for them. Soon others approached Eleutheros for legal work.

Making more than he'd ever earned in Madison, Eleutheros decided to settle in the area and, to that end, bought land in nearby Bloomingville. His business in New York kept him tied up well into 1818, so he didn't relocate to his new home until November. Making a former bank into his house, it was here in 1819 that his first son, Pitt, was born. Two years later, he relocated to Ogontz Place on Lake Erie's Sandusky Bay, a settlement named for the Ottawa chief who'd once lived there. Ogontz Place became Portland, then Sandusky City, then just Sandusky. It's here that Jay Cooke was born on August 10, 1821.

Jay Cooke later claimed that he knew Chief Ogontz and rode on his shoulders. Another story says that the chief visited periodically, camping in the barn and eating dinner with the family. Whoever this Ogontz was, it's not the one who lived here before Sandusky's founding. He was long dead by the time of Cooke's birth. Possibly Cooke knew Ogontz's grandson, a chief who lived by Lake Superior and did visit Ohio periodically.

In 1836, a fifteen-year-old Cooke was offered $600 to work at the Seymour and Bool's store in St. Louis. Accepting, he headed there that summer. At this time, St. Louis consisted of about 7,500 souls, most of them French and Indigenous people. Arriving before the store was completed, Cooke spent the next six weeks hunting in the wilderness.

Life here brought new experiences and opportunities. He visited the theater for the first time, went to dancing classes twice a week, attended writing school, improved his penmanship, and learned French. All went well until the Panic of 1837 heralded an economic depression that caused the Seymour and Bool shop to fail. Cooke returned home with $200 in his pocket (over $6,500 today), a fantastic sum for most American adults, let alone a fifteen-year-old boy.

Cooke's elder sister, Sarah, married William G. Moorehead, a businessman and politician. In 1838, Moorehead invited the sixteen-year-

Jay Cooke during the Civil War. Wenderoth & Taylor. From the December 1906 issue of *Century Magazine. Digitized by Google Books.*

old Cooke to come to Philadelphia to work as a clerk for his company, the Washington Packet Line, which ran freight between Philadelphia and Pittsburgh. Its failure a few months later prompted Cooke to return home for a second time. During his time in Philadelphia, he'd met and impressed bank owner Enoch W. Clark, and Clark enticed the youth to return to Philadelphia to work for his bank, E.W. Clark & Company, as a clerk. Cooke became a full partner in the bank by 1843 and took it over upon Clark's death in 1856.

Under Cooke's leadership, the bank prospered by investing in real estate and railroad bonds. Cooke did so well that he "retired" from banking in 1858, although that didn't stop him from putting together high-level deals. In 1861, he formed Jay Cooke & Co. with partners who included his brothers and Moorehead. When the Civil War broke out, Cooke, who'd always opposed slavery, embraced the Union cause. For the government he raised about $1.6 million by selling federal and state bonds. His firm made a fortune via insider trading, which wasn't outlawed until 1934. His bank famously tithed 10 percent of its profits to charitable causes.

After the war, Cooke used some of his fortune to purchase 250 acres in northwest Philadelphia, where he had a fifty-three-room mansion built surrounded by parks, gardens, and faux ruins. He named the estate Ogontz after his childhood friend. Near Sandusky, he bought the eight-acre Lake Erie island of Gibraltar, where he had a fifteen-room summer house called Cooke's Castle constructed.

He directed Jay Cooke & Co. to invest mainly in mining and oil drilling. Risk averse, in 1866 he decided not to involve the firm in the proposed Northern Pacific Railway. Chartered by Congress on July 2, 1864, it would connect Lake Superior at Duluth, Minnesota, to the Puget Sound at Tacoma in Washington Territory. The government gave the road public lands across which it could lay its tracks and allowed it to sell one million shares of stock. But there was a wee bit of a problem: a swath of the land over which it was

Plateau verging on the River of the Lakes and Mouse River
Extensive rolling prairies with ponds and marshes and nearly destitute of wood
500 miles
400 miles
300 miles
98° Longitude West from Greenwich
Rivière des Lacs
Mouse River
Shayenne River
PLATEAU DU COTEAU DU MISSOURI
Good water in numerous ponds
Rolling prairies with numerous small lakes and ponds
Camp Guthrie
Preliminary Sketch
OF THE
NORTHERN PACIFIC RAIL ROAD
EXPLORATION AND SURVEY
FROM St PAUL TO RIVIERE DES LACS
made in 1853-4 by
I. I. STEVENS
Governor of Washington Territory
STATUTE MILES
The firm dark lines are an approximate location of practicable Rail Road lines.
dotted probable
Wagner & McGuigan, Lith. Phil^a
98-688746

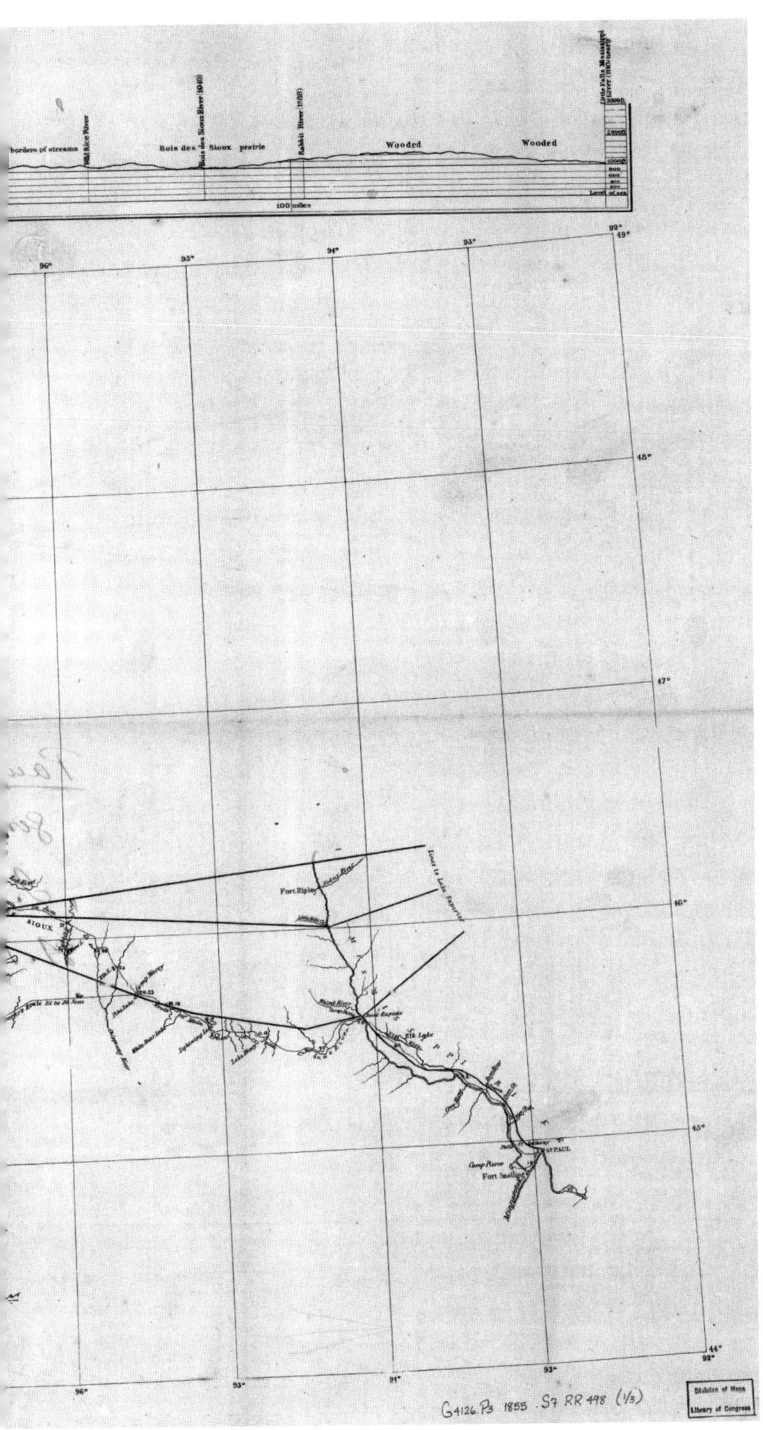

Isaac Ingalls Stevens made this preliminary sketch of the proposed Northern Pacific Railroad route in 1855. *Library of Congress Railroad Maps, 1828 to 1900.*

to be laid down was rough terrain already peopled by Indigenous groups hostile to the encroachment of Americans.

Cooke changed his mind about investing in the road in 1870. He began raising $5.5 million in bonds for it, increasing the goal to $13.5 million the next year. He financed the road's initial survey, which estimated that its two thousand miles of track would cost about $87,277,000 (over $2 billion today) to construct—a spectacular miscalculation. It didn't take long to incur massive overruns, and the expenses kept coming. Cooke poured his personal wealth into the venture to continue its financing. One of his partners, Harris C. Fahnestock, warned him not to get in so deep that it endangered the firm.

Construction on the eastern end of the Northern Pacific began near Duluth on February 15, 1870. Work began on the western part shortly thereafter. Extensive surveying was done in 1871, leaving just 225 miles to be done the next year. This last section proved particularly stubborn because it included Yellowstone Valley, prime hunting ground for the Sioux. In April 1871, Chief Sitting Bull, alarmed by surveying parties nearing territory controlled by his people, sent Spotted Eagle to Fort Sully in what is now central South Dakota to warn its commander, Colonel David Sloan Stanley, that his people would kill anyone entering the region and destroy any tracks laid down. Northern Pacific engineer-in-chief William Milnor Roberts thought this was an empty threat and said so publicly. The 1872 survey would go ahead.

Sitting Bull. W.S. Kimball & Co., 1888. *Library of Congress Prints and Photographs.*

It involved two parties, one coming from the east and the other from the west. The latter was headed by ex-Confederate engineering officer John A. Haydon, who'd spent a year of the Civil War in prisoner-of-war camp on Johnson's Island near Sandusky. Unlike Roberts, the U.S. Army did take Sitting Bull's threats seriously. A military escort commanded by Major Eugene Mortimer Baker would serve as the survey team's escort.

An 1859 graduate from West Point, Baker was an exceptional cavalry officer during the Civil War. He spent the first year of that conflict at Fort Churchill in Nevada. Returning to the East, he fought in the battles at Antietam and Gettysburg. Although a captain, he was breveted to major, then lieutenant colonel until the war's end. For a time, he served as an assistant

The Yellowstone River is a fast-moving body of water made even more dangerous during floods. Circa 1909 to 1932. *Library of Congress Prints and Photographs.*

adjutant general. In November 1865, he was sent out west, where he spent the remainder of his career. He was promoted to the rank of major in 1869. By this point, his addiction to alcohol had started impeding his ability to execute his duties, as we shall see.

Haydon's surveying party assembled at Fort Ellis at Bozeman, Montana Territory, and departed on July 27. The escort consisted of 376 officers and men supported by sixty-five ambulances, military wagons, and a herd of cattle. The soldiers and civilians in the surveying party numbered almost 500. They brought with them seven hundred animals. Heavy rains made it a miserable trek. Upon reaching the swollen Yellowstone River, they found it too deep and fast to cross where planned, forcing them to spend additional days looking for a more suitable ford. No surveying was done for the first sixteen days of the expedition.

At around 2:45 a.m. on August 14, Jack Gorman—a fugitive in the guise of a prospector who'd joined the expedition—woke and found a Sioux warrior trying to steal his rifle. Gorman shot the thief with his revolver.

More gunshots followed, alerting a group of officers playing poker that the camp was under attack. They sought out Baker but, finding him too drunk to give orders, dealt with the situation themselves.

According to a report written by Matt Caroll, who was in charge of transportation, roughly 450 warriors attacked with the primary goal of stealing mules. Pickets on guard fended the raiders off long enough for reinforcements to arrive. The fighting lasted about three hours, during which wagons were used as shields against bullets. Outgunned, the raiders departed. Two soldiers and one civilian died. Four were wounded.

Haydon called off the survey on August 19. The eastern expedition failed as well. This and the continued threat of the Sioux and their allies made it difficult for Jay Cooke & Co. to sell Northern Pacific bonds. Baker's drinking problem, it ought to be noted, didn't improve over the next decade. On July 5, 1881, he was court-martialed for drinking on duty. Found guilty, he was dismissed from the service. He died on December 19, 1884.

The overall prospects for raising the money needed to finance the Northern Pacific worsened in 1873. Europeans had invested heavily in American railroads, but by midsummer of that year, it became clear that land grants from the U.S. government had inflated their values. European banks with investments in them started collapsing under the weight of heavy debt not offset by the expected returns. Many American railroads teetered on the edge of bankruptcy. From October 1871 to May 1873, railroad loans couldn't be secured at rates less than 7 percent.

The first sign of an impending crash on Wall Street occurred in July, when the Brooklyn Trust Company temporarily closed, a victim of fraud by its president, Ethelbert S. Mills. The Warehouse & Security Company in New York City failed on September 8. Two of its directors, Sheppard Gandy and Francis Skiddy, both owned sugar importing companies. They found themselves in heavy debt after buying sugar at high prices and failing to corner the market as expected. A recent drop in the price of gold worsened the bank's position. Skiddy and Gandy were also directors of the Missouri–Kansas–Texas Railroad, then under construction and in need of money to continue operations. To finance their sugar venture, they'd borrowed a large sum against the railroad's bonds via the Warehousing & Security Company, and its inability to sustain this debt caused its closure. Few paid it attention. It was just another in a series of financial institutions brought down by fraud or mismanagement.

On September 16, New York City brokerage house Keynon, Cox & Company suspended operations. Its failure alarmed no one. It was the firm

Daniel Drew was initially blamed for the financial crash because of his previous intrigues involving railroad stock fraud. From *Harper's Magazine*, April 11, 1868. *Library of Congress Prints and Photographs.*

used by Daniel Drew, the notoriously corrupt financier and railroad mogul who was said to also be a partner in the firm. Its collapse was caused by a sudden drop in the stock price of the Toledo, Wabash & Western Railway and the failure of an investment in the Canadian Southern Railway. Rumor had it that Drew could have saved the firm with his personal fortune if he'd so chosen, but this was not true. A betrayal by business partners Jay Gould and James Fisk that cost him $1.5 million a few years earlier meant he didn't have that kind of wealth. The panic wiped him out, forcing him to declare bankruptcy in 1876. He spent his remaining days living with his son in modest circumstances.

Earlier in the year, a new Northern Pacific surveying party had headed to Yellowstone Valley to finish what the previous year's venture had failed to do. Its military escort, double in size, was led by Lieutenant Colonel George Custer, who'd been born in Ohio and raised both there and in Michigan. Always keen to inflate his reputation, he published his report of the expedition in the September 6 edition of the *New York Tribune*, in which he regaled readers with his great "victories" against the Sioux culminating at the Bighorn River on August 11. This was nothing more than a skirmish, but it had the effect of further spooking investment in the Northern Pacific.

By September, the Northern Pacific was no closer to becoming a true transcontinental railroad than when it was first proposed. While its western and eastern halves did have quite a lot of traffic, the amount of money spent to get it this far was too much for Jay Cooke & Co. On the morning of September 18, Fahnestock closed the firm's New York City branch, followed by the Philadelphia one a few hours later.

Its failure triggered runs on national banks with ties to the firm in the District of Columbia and Philadelphia, both of which survived. On September 20, more New York City banks failed: the Union Trust Company, Fisk & Hatch, the Mechanics' Banking Association, the Continental Bank, and the National Trust Company. Depositors demanded $60 million in cash withdrawals, money the banks didn't have.

Harris Charles Fahnestock is the one driving the carriage. The woman beside him may be his wife. The couple in the back are not identified. Circa 1890 to 1914. *Library of Congress Prints and Photographs.*

On that same day, President Grant and the secretary of the treasury, William Adams Richardson, arrived in the city where the latter started buying bonds and issuing loan certificates on behalf of the U.S. government. This had little effect on calming the panic. On September 20, the New York Stock Exchange closed for the first time in its history, and it didn't reopen for ten days.

Later in the year, Richardson issued a report about the panic's causes and the resulting economic depression. He considered its start on September 8 with the failure of the Warehouse & Security Company. The panic's root cause was that banks had overextended themselves with loans, especially ones to railroads. In the past five years, railroad investment alone amounted to $1.7 million, over $43 billion today. Many of the bonds and securities made available were sold to foreign markets, and when those stopped buying, the burden returned to a domestic market that couldn't support it. A panic was inevitable, and it was Jay Cooke & Co.'s ill luck to be its catalyst.

Cooke had to declare personal bankruptcy, during which both his Philadelphia house and his beloved vacation home on Gibraltar Island went

Above: The panic in New York City as seen on Broad and Nassau Streets. From *Frank Leslie's Illustrated Newspaper*, September 19, 1873. *Library of Congress Prints and Photographs.*

Left: Secretary of the Treasury William A. Richardson tried and failed to alleviate the initial panic. Circa 1870 to 1880. *Library of Congress Prints and Photographs.*

into receivership, although during their time in that state, no one offered to purchase them. Unlike Drew, Cooke was able to recover his fortune thanks to a sound investment in a Utah silver mine, giving him the money needed to regain control of Cooke's Castle and his Ogontz estate, the latter of which he never moved back into.

The rash of bank closures resulted in a string of railroad bankruptcies over the next few years. Of the 384 roads then in existence, 89 went into receivership, including the Northern Pacific in 1875. The Toledo, Wabash & Western failed that year as well, this being the Ohio railroad whose fallen stock price contributed to Keynon, Cox & Co.'s failure. The Toledo, Wabash & Western was first conceived in 1852 at a meeting in Toledo organized by Azariah Boody that consisted of Indiana and Ohio businessmen. The idea was to make Toledo the port where grain would be brought to Lake Erie, from which it would make its way across the Great Lakes, then down to the Mississippi Valley. The proposed railroad would cross the states of Ohio, Indiana, and Illinois to reach the Mississippi River.

Trying to create a single corporation in three states proved to be too difficult at this time, so its founders decided to incorporate one-half in Indiana and the other in Ohio. In 1856, the two roads merged into a single one named the Toledo, Wabash & Western Railroad. In 1858, suits by creditors forced it to split into two companies, both purchased by Boody in October of that year. The Ohio road became the Toledo & Wabash Railroad and the one in Indiana the Wabash & Western Railway Company. In 1865, several more roads joined the two separated ones to become the reconstituted Toledo, Wabash & Western Railway.

It absorbed the Decatur & East St. Louis Railway on February 1, 1873. To pay for it, the company issued $5 million in gold bonds and took out a mortgage on all its property and equipment. When one of its creditors, Metropolitan National Bank, demanded payment on June 29, 1875, it was refused because the road was in receivership. The next year, a judge ordered the sale of all its equipment and assets to pay its debts. John W. Ellis and others bought all its property on June 10 the next year. Out of this chaos, a new railroad, the Wabash Railway Company, was created on January 3, 1877.

By that year, half of America's railroads had gone into receivership. At this time, railroads were the biggest economic driver in America, so when the massive construction of new railroad lines and the equipment needed for them virtually stopped after the panic, it affected other industrial sectors. One was iron production, which fell nearly 45 percent within a year, and because demand by mills had fallen so much, many either closed or ran at reduced hours. The Panic of 1873 marks the starting point of the United States' first industrial economic depression, out of which it wouldn't climb until 1879.

CHAPTER 2
A PLAGUE OF TRAMPS

Ohio was hit especially hard by the depression. Wages here fell 29 percent for skilled laborers and 40 for unskilled ones. The price for groceries, by contrast, dropped just 12 percent, meaning those lucky to have work still couldn't afford to buy a sufficient amount to eat. Employers often held back pay between one and four months. Some paid in scrip that could only be redeemed at a company store, which sold goods at higher prices than elsewhere. Outside the company store, scrip was often only worth half of its face value by places willing to accept it, and against greenbacks the exchange rate was 40 percent. Those earning scrip often had company housing for which they paid rent, putting workers into further debt.

By 1875, an estimated three million men had no work, and of those who did, only about one-fifth worked year-round. Wages for the employed dropped so far that some made as little as a dollar a day, which no one could live on even in an era when a penny could get you far more than today. It also affected miners and, to a lesser extent, farmers, the latter unable to either get mortgages or afford the ones they had.

Desperate for work, an estimated 1.5 to 2 million men took to the road looking for it. Impoverished, they often illegally rode on freight trains and thieved when necessary. At a glance, they looked like unsavory characters because of their patched clothes, unwashed bodies, and unshaven faces. "Tramp," with all its negative connotations, first appeared in print in 1760. The word is a synonym for vagrant.

What the majority of these so-called tramps wanted was work. Its shortage was exacerbated by businesses that decided to keep costs down by replacing

A pair of tramps walking down some train tracks. Bain News Service. Date unknown. *Library of Congress Prints and Photographs.*

adults with children. In Chicago, for example, boys hired to be upholsters earned between three and five dollars a week, three times less than the average for adults. Their workplaces were dust-filled, a condition that could be improved, except businesses didn't want to incur the extra cost to do so.

Silver gilders had it no better. Their workspaces had insufficient heat in the winter and closed windows in the summer, forcing workers to breathe in poisonous vapors. Shoemakers complained that competition with convict labor had put 250 of them out of work in Chicago alone.

Making matters worse was the Coinage Act of 1873, which effectively put the United States back on the gold standard by forbidding the U.S. Mint from striking silver coins. It caused the price of silver to plummet, which affected the average person who possessed mainly paper money or silver. It also sparked a fierce debate over modifying the law, and in 1876, Ohio Congressman Thomas Ewing Jr. and New York Governor Stewart L. Woodford had a series of debates throughout Ohio about this. Woodford wanted to keep the gold standard, and Ewing wanted to shift to a bimetal system where the value of the dollar was based on both gold and silver. Republicans like Woodford feared a bimetal system would cause inflation.

Ewing, born on August 7, 1829, came from a well-to-do family in Lancaster, Ohio. His first political job was serving as one of President Zachary Taylor's private secretaries. After that, he studied law, and for a time he practiced in Leavenworth, Kansas, where he also did some land speculating. An active member of the Kansas Free State Party, he helped uncover the fraud used by proslavery state officers to get elected in 1855, forcing them out and allowing Kansas to enter the Union as a free state.

During the Civil War, he joined the Union army and rose to the rank of brevet major general. Throughout that conflict, he opposed the use of Black troops, and after the war, he supported President Andrew Johnson's policies for Reconstruction that aimed to restore the slaveholding class's grip on post-Confederate governments. Returning to Lancaster in 1870, Ewing switched to the Democratic Party and joined the Clement L. Vallandigham wing, which sought to realign the country's divisions from North–South to East–West.

During one of his debates with Governor Woodford over the money issue, Ewing turned to the topic of tramps:

> *And the records of Perry County* [Ohio] *will show that over half the men that bought their homes there have lost them in two years past, and those who still have them are suffering foreclosures and sales for the third or two-thirds balance of purchase money. From those mining and manufacturing communities were sent out the men whom Republican orators and newspapers denounce and scoff at as tramps....In my own town of Lancaster*[,] *our little jail was filled many nights with stalwart,*

Left: Thomas Ewing Jr. during the Civil War. Brady's National Photographic Portrait Galleries. Circa 1860 to 1865. *Library of Congress Prints and Photographs.*

Right: Stewart L. Woodford. Circa 1870 to 1880. *Library of Congress Prints and Photographs.*

> *sober young men—filled so that in some of those inclement nights they had not room to lie down; seeking the jail at night to keep from freezing, and walking by day from town to town.*

Never before had massive poverty appeared so publicly. Although states did have some institutions to deal with the poor, the federal government never considered it and wouldn't until President Franklin D. Roosevelt implemented the New Deal. Americans on the whole opposed the federal government giving individual Americans any kind of aid, considering it undemocratic because it favored one group over another.

Relief, such as it was, came from a patchwork of private charities and state- or county-run public assistance programs that didn't communicate with one another, and those at the top in these organizations didn't bother to meet with the very people they espoused to help. For private charities, the aim was to help the "deserving poor." Founders of charities had a pathological fear that paupers gamed the system, a belief reinforced by newspaper reports of fraud.

Those running the charities were usually the college-educated elite whose goal wasn't to alleviate poverty but to encourage spiritual improvement. Religious leaders, reformers, and politicians who embraced so-called scientific charity believed in a twisted misinterpretation of Charles Darwin's theory of evolution that claimed poverty was biological and therefore inherited, making helping those in need a pointless effort. Others greatly feared that giving aid would make the poor dependent on it.

Those who attended the Conference of Charities in Saratoga Springs, New York, in September 1877 had little charity in their hearts. At the conference, Reverend Edward E. Hale suggested that American society had decided feeding hungry people was the right thing to do and there was no convincing them it would be better to let the poor starve. He suggested "that we create this army of tramps by the lavishness with which we feed them; that so long as a nation gave away food as readily as it gave air or water, there would be lazy dogs ready to take it on as easy terms." He believed a story he'd heard that a man who'd never worked a day in his life had successfully begged for the past eighteen years and would do so until his dying day. Hale acknowledged that Americans weren't going to stand by and allow people to starve to death on the streets, so his solution was to put tramps and other impoverished people into county workhouses. This was hardly a novel suggestion.

This engraving of Reverend Edward E. Hale is based on a photograph by George Collins Cox. Circa 1884. *Library of Congress Prints and Photographs.*

People believed that tramps refused to work, an excuse given by those in a position to help who refused to do so. Two Massachusetts reporters went undercover and traveled with different groups of tramps. They wrote, "The usual question to the young tramp is, 'Why don't you go to work?' They always profess readiness to work, but generally give, as a trade to which they are accustomed to work, some occupation in which they are sure no employment will be offered in that locality." Here the point was missed. Tramps were, by definition, men on the move looking for work in their chosen trade, whatever it might be.

The July 1878 issue of *Fire Lands Pioneer* magazine reprinted an article from the *Sandusky Register* that editorialized, "It is probably correct to say that no one tramp in a hundred is a man of family, has anybody dependent on him for support, or cares a continental for anyone but himself. Most of them, as a matter of fact, are young men from eighteen to twenty-five years of age who were single." The article failed to mention that the reason most out-of-work laborers were single was because they were laid off before married men.

Which isn't to say married men weren't among their ranks. George Rogers, an iron molder by trade, had a wife and children. For a time, he was forced to tramp across Ohio and Michigan in search of work. Sometimes farmers provided him with food. Others set dogs on him. In Michigan, some wouldn't give him a drink just because he was a tramp. When asked why he didn't go into another trade, he replied it was because iron molding was what he did.

As further "evidence" that tramps refused to work, the *Register* cited its own experience. It had gone through twenty compositors in the past five years, none of whom lasted more than a week. With that kind of turnover rate during an economic depression, one wonders just how bad that job must have been.

Few newspapers were sympathetic to tramps or their plight, and the *New York Times* was no different. In an 1876 article titled "The Tramp Convention," it reported that tramps across the United States were heading to Cleveland for a convention. There they would demand "fewer large dog-houses" and call for "the formation of a union and the adoption of a scale of diet. If a skilled tramp is to flourish and grow fat, he must crush out the rivalry of mean-spirited tramps who accept cheap and plain food." Only mocha coffee, as an example, would do. Such satire was unusual for the *New York Times*.

Authorities saw no difference between tramps and professional criminals. In November 1886, there was a series of burglaries in Greenfield, Ohio. In one incident, someone broke into the house of Harrison Dent while he and his family were out. They lived about a mile and a half outside of town on a farm owned by John Stewart through which the Marietta & Cincinnati Railroad's tracks went. Upon returning home, the Dennis family found their front door broken open and a number of items stolen, including boots, clothes, two razors, and about twenty-five pounds of flour.

Police suspected the robbers were "tramps" camping in Mitchell's Woods to the west of town. Stewart, three policemen, and Ed Arthur, who was armed with a double-barreled shotgun, pursued the suspects in the direction of New Vienna. The posse found them camped about a mile from the Marietta & Cincinnati's tracks. Upon surrounding the encampment, those within ran for it, each throwing a pack as he did so. Most were caught. Nothing was found incriminating on any one person, but their packs contained stolen goods. Another suspect was arrested as the officers headed back to New Vienna. Those apprehended were Arthur Chambers, Frank Wilson, James Mason, Joe Coburn, Thomas Laughlin, and Tom Allen. The reporter who wrote the article from which this information comes thought the names were probably assumed, as were the men's claims of where they'd come from.

If their names were aliases, they stuck with them throughout their court case. Laughlin was from Buffalo, New York, and had left years earlier. The gang's leader was, by his own admission, a criminal who hadn't worked an honest job in the last five years. All six pleaded guilty to burglary. Save for Laughlin, they all claimed this was the first time they'd been arrested and asked the judge for mercy. He had none. He said that they were an organized gang that roamed about stealing, and he wanted them locked up. But because they pleaded guilty, he'd be "lenient" and sentence them to *only* five years of hard labor. The defendants had expected sentences of one to two years.

The Ohio legislature became so alarmed about the number of tramps traveling about that it assembled an advisory committee of politicians and community leaders in Columbus to determine who qualified as a tramp and what should be done with this group. Mr. Sherman of Lima thought they should be compelled to work, and to that end, a state law ought to be passed. Chris Lewis from Columbus was reluctant to class anyone impoverished and on the road as a tramp. He asserted that many an honest man had, because of circumstance beyond his control, been forced to beg. He knew hundreds of men considered tramps who would happily work given the chance.

Mr. Elliott of Milford Center wanted measures implemented to rid the country of them. Another attendee believed it was folly to argue about who was a tramp because it was clear they were all tramps and beggars by choice. An honest man could get something to do, at least sufficient to make a living. Mr. Coit from Columbus, in contrast, was sure the tramp issue would end when business revived, so only temporary measures were needed. In the end, the committee recommended to the Ohio legislature that if tramps refused to find jobs, they'd be locked up and forced to work. The committee further called for the creation of workhouses and the passage of laws making vagrancy illegal. No measure of outright relief should be offered, and it might be desirable to put tramps in a chain gang.

After learning about the committee and its recommendation, the Chicago newspaper *Workingman's Advocate* wrote a stinging rebuke. It pointed out that most of those who made up the committee "were village, town, and county officials and lawyers—men whose very vocation proves them to be paupers. They produce nothing, and live off what the public sees fit to give them as charity," which they call their salary. If they lost their income, they'd become tramps themselves. Tens of thousands of men were unemployed through no fault of their own, and now they roamed the country looking for the very work that others claimed they refused to take.

An editorial by Milton Allen that appeared in the December 20, 1877 edition of the *Tiffin Tribune* had a more nuanced take on the issue. Allen estimated that Ohio had about twenty-five thousand tramps but realized the majority were men thrown out of work. He agreed that some of them were criminals or drifters but figured most wanted neither alms nor charity; it offended their personal dignity.

Many Ohio municipalities implemented the committee's recommendations. The city of Springfield, as an example, passed a law against vagrancy on January 18, 1876. Citizens of the city who had no means of support could present themselves to a police station and there receive lodging and food at the city's expense in exchange for an equal amount of labor under the direction of the street commissioner. Well, this is precisely what many of these unemployed people wanted! Those who refused to work would be charged with vagrancy and, if convicted, pay no more than a fifty-dollar fine plus be imprisoned, sent to the workhouse for hard labor, or both. It was up to a court to decide.

The tactic of arresting people for vagrancy addressed only a symptom of the problem. The federal government did nothing to deal with the depression, and the response from states was tepid at best. Radical ideas ignored or dismissed during the post–Civil War boom suddenly gained traction with the working class. In 1877, Congress created a select committee to investigate the causes of the depression, and while in Chicago it interviewed both businessmen and workers, the latter espousing ideas that few elected officials dared embrace.

D.R. Streeter, a printer and representative of a council of trade and labor, said his group believed their ills were caused because many men had been replaced by automation. The government should take ownership of all machines and workers get four-fifths of the profits generated by the businesses for which they worked. An eight-hour day should be adopted. All children under the age of fourteen should be compelled to attend school, which in addition to giving them an education had the added benefit of preventing them from competing with adults for work. The government should prohibit employers from using prison labor, introduce a graduated income tax, protect the right to strike, and implement sanitary inspections.

Another printer interviewed by the select panel, P.H. McLogan, said the wages in his trade had dropped by half from 1872 to 1879. He, too, wanted an eight-hour day and suggested that since the U.S. government subsidized railroads, it likewise should do so for workers. He believed most tramps were out-of-work men looking for work and dismissed the idea that they should head out west for the free land on offer there. What good would it do them if they didn't have money to buy the equipment needed to work it?

Clearly these men had been influenced by the socialist and communist ideas then becoming popular, although communal settlements had been present since the nation's founding. Often inspired by the churches founded by Saint Paul in which everything was owned collectively, these utopian groups sent waves of terror through those whose god was private property. Journalist Charles Nordhoff visited many of these settlements. He reported what he'd found in his 1875 book, *The Communist Societies of the United States.* Included in it were Economy, Pennsylvania (founded by the Harmony Society); Oneida, New York (founded by the free-love Perfectionists); the Shakers (who had multiple communities); and Zoar Village in Ohio.

This last had its roots in the German kingdom of Württemberg, where a group who referred to themselves as Separatists wanted no part of the state-run Lutheran Church because they didn't believe in a hierarchal religion. With help from English and American Quakers, they immigrated to America in 1817. Joseph Michael Bäumler, who later Anglicized his last name to Bimeler, became their leader during their harrowing sea voyage.

The Separatists numbered seventy-eight women and sixty-seven men plus children. They bought 5,500 acres of land in Tuscarawas County sight unseen from German Moravian land dealer Godfrey Haga. During their first year, everyone had a private plot and survived without help from their fellow Separatists. This was especially hard on the elderly members. Others were forced to work for non-Separatists to make ends meet. In an effort to succeed, they decided to share everything communally. Bimeler initially opposed it because he worried the selfishness of some members would doom it to failure, but being familiar with the success of the communal society at Economy, he decided to try it. All members signed articles of agreement on April 15, 1819, which created the Society of Separatists of Zoar.

This new model worked well beyond expectations. For economic reasons, members remained celibate from 1822 to 1828. Marriage was forbidden. They raised cattle, grew crops, and started up the kind of shops needed for any community of that era, including a blacksmith, joiner, and carpenter. In 1827, the Ohio & Erie Canal opened through their land, allowing them to easily get their animals and crops to market. They opened several mills, a woolen factory, a store, and, in 1833, a hotel.

Nordhoff had little good to say about them, calling them peasants from southern Germany who read little save for the Bible. He pointed out that their village still lacked paved sidewalks, its houses needed paint, and the place was overall shabby. He was surprised they'd prospered at all considering that they had a "dull and lethargic appearance." He did concede that they had the best sheep, cattle, and horses in Tuscarawas County.

Many who read Nordhoff's book saw Zoar Village as a beacon of hope—a successful enterprise despite the hard times. People wrote the village asking for information and even membership. For some the draw was religious; for others it was communism. Many wanted to visit to see it for themselves. It also attracted former Shakers, one of whom, Amasa Blodgett, was accepted as a member—the only non-German adult allowed to join. So many people wrote asking how they could become a member that the Society had to create a form rejection letter.

Even during the 1870s depression, Zoar was a popular tourist destination. The arrival of the Wheeling & Lake Erie Railroad* brought in many day-trippers. So popular did the village become that in 1891 Zoar's Standing Committee and trustees proposed building an addition to Zoar Hotel because it couldn't accommodate all the visitors. Built in the Queen Anne style, the annex had conveniences such as modern plumbing and hot baths.

Tourism was one of the contributing factors to Zoar's undoing. Most Society members worked to support it because Zoar's industries hadn't kept up with technological advances, and the money wasn't there to invest in them. The worldly goods brought in by tourists such as buggies and fashionable clothes were a temptation too great to overcome. As the third-generation Society members came of age, they not only lacked the

* This is the only Ohio railroad mentioned in this book that still operates under its original name.

Zoar Hotel, date unknown. *Library of Congress Prints and Photographs.*

experience of religious persecution in Germany, but they also didn't see what was so appealing about sharing everything.

Society members employed in places like the hotel earned their own money in the form of tips. Only about one-third of them attended Sunday services. Between 1884 and 1887, the Society nearly went bankrupt. Because the majority of younger members desired it, a decision to end the commune was made in 1898. Save for a few places such as the cemetery and town hall, all assets were divided among the members.

CHAPTER 3

WORKING ON THE RAILROAD

Possibly no industry has been more romanticized than railroads. But beneath this sheen lurks an unpleasant reality. For much of its history, its workers were treated as a disposable commodity to be paid the bare minimum so profits would be maximized for shareholders. Even in good times, train crewmen rarely worked a consistent number of hours each month. Peak seasons were spring and fall, the latter because harvests needed to be transported. Bad weather could also result in reduced hours.

With the onset of the depression, men might be employed only three days a week, yet were expected to be on call the other four. When they did work, they were stranded at the end point of their run. The railroad paid for neither their ticket home on a passenger train nor their hotel stay, the latter usually being at a higher-priced railroad-owned establishment. Heavy indebtedness to one's road could result in wages being garnished and even dismissal.

Most crewmen worked between ten and twelve hours a day, sometimes more, and were forced to perform unpaid labor. Engineers earned money only while in the cab, not for all the things they needed to do to maintain their engines. Firemen had to spend hours each day cleaning the engine. It wasn't unknown on the Pennsylvania Railroad for firemen and engineers to pay for the repairs to their locomotives out of their own pockets. They earned nothing during the sometimes lengthy period repairs took to complete.

It ought to be noted that while train freight crews were exclusively male in the 1870s, women also worked for railroads, primarily in occupations

Above: You can tell this locomotive is used for a passenger train because it has large wheels. Freight train engines had small wheels to give them more torque. Detroit Publishing Company, circa 1904. *Library of Congress Prints and Photographs.*

Opposite: Justin G. Cooper, railroad fireman. National Photo Company, circa 1918–20. *Library of Congress Prints and Photographs.*

such as clerical work, selling tickets, and operating telegraphs. One female telegrapher was Elizabeth Cogley. She began working for the Pennsylvania Railroad on April 13, 1856. On April 16, 1861, she made history by being the first person to receive and transcribe a telegraphed message from President Abraham Lincoln calling for troops to defend the Union. Cogley worked for the Pennsylvania Railroad for over forty years.

Telegraphy wasn't an easy occupation, and male chauvinists of the day didn't think women could do it. Railroads decided to give them a chance anyway, mainly because they could pay them less. The average day lasted over ten hours. The locations in which they worked were often in the middle of nowhere, making it a lonely job and not one without risk. Working in poorly ventilated enclosed spaces increased the risk of contracting diseases like tuberculosis, usually a slow and painful death sentence in those days.

Being a telegrapher could also be deadly. Lizzie Clapp, a telegrapher for the Boston & Providence Railroad, was killed on July 11, 1876, while performing her duties. As a thunderstorm rolled through, lightning struck the telegraph line and jumped to her gold necklace, electrocuting her. She was eighteen years old.

Some women were railroad architects. Quite a few invented improvements for the rail system or trains. Mary Walton devised a way to reduce the amount of smoke engines emitted by pushing it through a water tank (an idea never implemented) and reduced the noise of elevated trains in New York City by filling their support boxes with cotton or sand—a solution even Thomas Edison had failed to discover. Eliza Murfey invented a lubrication device that helped prevent derailments. Mary Isabelle Riggin invented the railroad crossing gate. Catherine Gibbon streamlined and improved the construction of tracks.

Railroads had employee manuals written for train crews outlining their roles and the strict rules they had to follow. Not doing so could result in dismissal. Although rules varied by company, the April 1878 manual from the Eastern Railway Company—a road that ran from Boston, Massachusetts, to Portland, Maine—gives a good idea of the duties of the train and support crews.

This manual stressed safety in general and that of passengers above all else. To that end, employees were forbidden from smoking or drinking on the job. Those who appeared intoxicated while on duty would be removed from the train and probably fired. Employees couldn't leave their posts without permission from the appropriate superior.

A train's top crewman was the conductor. In addition to being responsible for its safety and movement along the road, he made sure that all subordinates performed their assigned tasks, and he assumed responsibility for their misconduct. Conductors were accountable for all equipment used on a train, including flags, signal lanterns, pins, and spare coupling links. They were required to carry an accurate watch with the correct time. Conductors and engineers were responsible for obeying speed laws inside municipalities. If fined for a violation, they paid it out of their own pocket.

Railroads made their money hauling freight, not passengers. Freight crews consisted of the conductor, engineer, fireman, and brakemen. Of these, the brakemen had the most dangerous job. Freight trains were stopped one car at a time with a wheel turned to engage the brake located at its top. The engineer indicated he wanted his brakemen to start slowing the train using a coded whistle. To execute this, they leapt between the tops of swaying cars, the gap between them ranging from twenty-seven to thirty inches. The brakemen's chance of falling increased exponentially during the night or when the weather turned foul.

Brakemen also had to be mindful of overpasses. A strike against one of these was usually fatal. Massachusetts tried to alleviate this danger by mandating the erection of overhanging "guards" that would rap against the tops of the cars to warn brakemen of the oncoming obstacle. Brakemen found them so annoying that they often took them down, compelling the Massachusetts legislature to pass a law making doing so a crime.

A train with thirteen cars moving sixty miles an hour took half a mile to halt. Few braking systems existed that allowed an engineer to stop the train himself, and those that did were held in reserve for emergencies and weren't effective. That changed when a twenty-one-year-old inventor named George Westinghouse filed a patent for airbrakes on July 10, 1868.

George Westinghouse. Bain News Service, date unknown. *Library of Congress Prints and Photographs.*

The airbrakes worked like this. Each car had a reservoir of compressed air controlled by three valves. When the engineer pulled a lever in the engine's cab, that engaged a piston that pushed the brakes onto the wheels. The system was connected from the engine to the rest of the train via a series of pipes and hoses, giving the engineer the ability to stop all the cars simultaneously with the pull of a lever from the cab. Westinghouse filed over one hundred patents improving on his invention. One of the most important was the one that caused the brakes to automatically engage if the air pressure from the engine to the cars was disrupted. They would, as an example, be triggered by a derailment.

Inventing an ingenious system was one thing, but selling it to railroads was quite another. Most railroad executives didn't think much of

Westinghouse's new device and refused to so much as test it. Then, out of the blue came an offer to test the brakes from W.W. Card, the man who oversaw the Steubenville, Ohio division of the Pittsburgh, Columbus, Cincinnati & St. Louis Railroad. This part of the road, a subsidiary of the Pennsylvania Railroad, was known as the Panhandle because it crossed the northern panhandle of West Virginia on its route between Pennsylvania and Ohio. In its offer, the Panhandle stipulated that it wouldn't finance the test or pay for any damages. Westinghouse and his financial backer, Ralph Baggaley, agreed to this. The two financed the installation of the brakes themselves.

The test began when a single locomotive pulling four cars driven by engineer Daniel Tate started from Pittsburgh on its way to Steubenville. As the train came out of the Grant Tunnel in Pittsburgh doing thirty miles per hour, trouble occurred. Two blocks away on Second Avenue, the horses of a wagon crossing the tracks panicked, throwing the driver onto the tracks. Tate engaged the airbrakes, and the train halted just four feet before the driver. This so impressed the Pennsylvania Railroad that it immediately started putting the brakes on its passenger trains. It could have put them on freight trains as well but declined to do so because it deemed it too expensive.

Another cost-saving measure was to run trains in both directions on a single track rather than using a more costly double-track system, and here the Panhandle was no different. At 11:47 p.m. on August 6, 1878, one of its passenger trains driven by engineer James Dugan pulled out of Pittsburgh and headed west. Dugan's train consisted of two postal, one baggage, two sleeper, one hotel, and two coach cars, with the last carrying newly arrived immigrants. At the same time, a Panhandle freight train in Ohio driven by engineer Charles Graham was heading east on the same track. Its conductor, William Storing, didn't realize his watch had stopped, so his train was between fifteen and twenty minutes behind schedule.

Both trains entered a narrow *S*-shaped valley that followed the contours of Cross Creek near Mingo Junction, a small Ohio settlement five miles south of Steubenville. The valley had steep hills covered with a thick forest of trees, making it largely inaccessible from either side. The tracks sat atop a high embankment. A dense fog lessened visibility. When the two engineers saw one another, Dugan slammed on the airbrakes and slowed his train considerably. Not having that ability, Graham's train rushed ahead at about forty miles per hour and slammed head-on with the other. Had both trains been equipped with airbrakes, the two might have slowed well enough to avoid the catastrophe that resulted.

The collision violently awoke H.E. Havens of Springfield, Missouri, who was in a sleeper car. A railroad man, he'd just come from Washington, D.C. He pulled on his pants and prepared to jump out, but the car stopped moving before he did so. He heard smashing sounds and then people screaming and groaning. He and others immediately started rendering what assistance they could. The only light available came from a single lantern. A surviving crewman, either a brakeman or conductor, tried to send a telegraph from nearby Mingo Junction, but unable to find an operator, he had to run at full speed toward Steubenville to find help.

Havens told the *St. Louis Globe-Democrat* that he and others "found a great many people with legs cut to pieces, both sometimes, and heads smashed." Most of those injured were immigrants from the coaches, many of whom couldn't speak English. Havens helped rescue Graham from the wreck of his locomotive, which had slid down the embankment along with the passenger train's engine. Graham would live. The other train's engineer, Dugan, died shortly after his extraction.

About fifteen minutes after the crash, five men carrying lanterns who'd heard the sound of the collision arrived to give what assistance they could. Havens claimed that passengers who suffered no injuries returned to their berths, which he attributed to "great inhumanity or else great cowardice," but more likely it was shock. A special train arrived in the morning on which "four or five doctors, and about fifteen other men, including policemen," came.

The postal car had plunged about thirty feet down the embankment, smashing it into pieces and killing postal clerks W. Johnston, A.W. Andrews, and Frank D. Graham. A fourth postal worker, George L. Moreau, survived but suffered a broken leg. In addition to Dugan and the three postal workers, fourteen others were killed or injured. This is one of the few cases in which the brakemen came out nearly unscathed because they were in the caboose at the time of the crash. The freight train's conductor later said had he realized how late his train was, he would have waited for the other one to pass.

In addition to stopping trains, brakemen were also responsible for coupling and uncoupling cars. A link-and-pin system was used that compelled them to stand between cars to connect the drawbars. Rarely did these fit well, especially when cars came from different manufacturers. Many veteran brakemen were missing one or more of their fingers.

They often had to run alongside cars, and a trip, fall, or misstep could be deadly. This happened in Colton, Ohio, to William Moest at the end of March 1875. When he was working for the Toledo, Wabash & Western Railroad, his foot was trapped by a frog—the moving part of a track that shifts when it switches—and before he could extricate himself, he was knocked down. Three cars ran over him, cutting his body in half and leaving a gruesome mess.

A better alternative to the link and pin existed. The knuckle-coupler was patented in 1873. This way of linking cars was controlled by a handle to lock and unlock a coupler, allowing the cars to connect and disconnect without fingers getting in the way. Railroads didn't adopt it universally until the federal Railroad Safety Act of 1893 required it. This same act also made installing airbrakes on all trains compulsory.

Even with airbrakes, trains in the nineteenth century were just plain dangerous. George L. Vose examined this reality in an October 1882 *North American Review* article titled "Safety in Railway Travel." Admitting that the statistics available were incomplete, he estimated in that year alone, "there were one hundred thousand miles of railroads completed and in operation, employing not less than half a million persons, and transporting annually about three hundred and seventy-five millions of passengers." Each year about one thousand serious accidents occurred, and he guessed no fewer than ten thousand people were injured or killed annually, be they workers, passengers, or bystanders hit by trains.

The *Annual Report of the Commissioner of Railroad and Telegraphs* for Ohio covering the period between June 30, 1867, and June 30, 1868, provides some good examples of the types of accidents railroads caused. The Atlantic & Great Western Railway reported that five employees and one non-employee were killed. Injuries amounted to twenty-eight for employees, eight for passengers, and four for bystanders.

The Cincinnati & Indiana Railroad had a dismal year that was especially hard on its employees. Jerry Halpin's arm was crushed while he was coupling cars in Cincinnati. Charles Pennock's arm was broken in Cincinnati while he coupled cars. Dennis Sullivan stepped on the track in front of a moving train and was killed. William Sullivan was "slightly injured while coupling cars" in Cleves.

Bystanders and riders also suffered. A train hit and killed nine-year-old Hamlet Sykes as he sat on the tracks fastening on his skates. A train rear-ended another one, resulting in the injury of three passengers. A man was killed while walking on the tracks near Sedamsville. A train struck and killed James McNeal "one mile east of Delhi [Township]."

In addition to human casualties, the Central Ohio Railroad reported that its trains killed thirty-four cows, six steers, eleven calves, five hogs, sixty-two sheep, nine horses, and one colt. The saddest part of this is that the amount

Cowcatcher with a knuckle-coupler. Engine 1551. Age of Steam Roundhouse, Sugarcreek, Ohio. *Photo taken by the author.*

of compensation given to the owners of these dead animals amounted to zero. Most if not all of these animals probably met their deaths at the end of the so-called cowcatcher, which did no such thing. Made of iron, this piece of hardware was designed to prevent derailment by smashing through anything that got in the engine's way, be it animal, person, or vehicle.

Railroad workers injured or the widows of those killed had little hope of receiving the barest of compensation. Sometimes railroads did cover the cost of hospitals or funerals, but it depended on company policy. No form of insurance existed, nor would any start until the 1880s. If taken to court, railroads usually won. At this time, judges accepted the common law that those who worked for another agreed to take all risks, including negligence by fellow employees.

Railroad safety laws even at the state level were few and far between. Ohio had no government inspectors of railway bridges or laws stipulating standards for their construction. As a result, the bridges had a habit of collapsing, usually with trains on them. Such an incident occurred around 8:30 a.m. on Thursday, December 12, 1867, in Fremont, Ohio. An unexpected blizzard with gale-force winds and heavy snowfall prompted the engineer, Mr. Brannon, to slow down his ten-car Toledo & Cleveland Railroad freight train pulled by the engine *Elyria* before crossing the Sandusky River via a recently winterized stone arch bridge covered with an iron roof.

In this photo taken of the Sandusky River in Fremont, Ohio, the bridge in the background belonged to the Lake Erie & Western Railroad. From a postcard printed in Great Britain, circa 1907–15. *Author's collection.*

As the train passed over, the bridge's roof blew off, striking and knocking the train off the tracks east of the center pier. This caused the bridge's entire eastern section to collapse. The *Elyria* somersaulted as it fell and crashed into the east pier, which knocked it into pieces. The tender was thrown onto the river's east bank. The *Fremont Weekly Journal* reported that a car "loaded with dressed hogs was thrown forty or fifty feet up the river and lies partly out of the water." The caboose with four men and one freight car stayed on the tracks, while another car landed on timbers.

After the engine hit the water, Brannon and the fireman jumped into the river, which was shallow. They made it to the house of Mr. Ginn, at which they took refuge from the storm. Bannon had three broken ribs, bruising, and some internal injuries. The fireman suffered a cut on his head. Conductor William Carver from Bellevue disappeared, his body being found that Saturday. Crews had to wait until the storm abated before recovery, cleanup, and repairs were possible. A temporary bridge was constructed by a crew of seventy men in just five days. A more permanent wooden one would take about six weeks to build. It was believed the bridge's pillars collapsed because the arches were too small to bear the bridge's load.

One of Ohio's worst train bridge collapses occurred on December 29, 1876, when the bridge failure over the Ashtabula River in Ashtabula

The collapsed railroad bridge seen here belonged to the Cleveland, Mount Vernon & Columbus Railroad and crossed the Big Walnut Creek near Sunbury, Ohio. 1881. *Library of Congress Prints and Photographs.*

County resulted in the passenger train crossing it to plummet sixty-nine feet to the bottom of a gully. This crash resulted in the official death count of around ninety-two plus countless injuries. On October 17, 1879, a bridge over the Big Walnut Creek near Sunbury, Ohio, collapsed as a Cleveland, Mount Vernon & Columbus Railroad freight train crossed. The fall of forty feet resulted in the injury of five crewmen. The bridge was rebuilt, but its replacement failed in 1912 and had to be reconstructed as well.

With all the dangers railroad workers faced, the railway companies had still another way to increase the chances of an accident or death: the doubleheader. Used for freight and coal trains, this was the doubling of car engines with the same number of crewmen. Regular freight and coal trains on the Pennsylvania Railroad, for example, consisted of one engine and eighteen cars, so a doubleheader had thirty-six cars with an engine on either end. It doubled the crew's risk, and as we shall see in chapter 6, they weren't just going to accept it.

CHAPTER 4

THE STRIKE BEGINS

With the depression cutting so deeply into business, the eastern and midwestern U.S. railroads made compacts with one another to set freight rates that were soon violated on the sly to gain more business. In March 1877, William H. Vanderbilt, president of the New York Central Railroad, accused the Baltimore & Ohio Railroad of breaking its latest pledge. Hugh J. Jewett, the Erie Railroad's receiver, said he'd take business at whatever rate he could get it because he'd gotten sick of making compacts broken before being implemented. All major roads claimed they'd kept to their agreements but their competitors hadn't. In mid-May, the Baltimore & Ohio's president, John W. Garrett, called a meeting of railroad representatives to New York City's Brevoort Hotel to settle the matter by getting the eastern roads to maintain the same rates. This came to nothing.

The depression and this rate war caused the Baltimore & Ohio's revenue to shrink by 62 percent between 1873 and 1877. Despite this, it paid a 10 percent dividend to its stockholders every year between 1873 and 1876. Garrett planned to do so again in 1877. To finance it, he announced that effective July 16, workers' wages would be reduced by 10 percent, this on top of the previous year's 10 percent cut. Now firemen and brakemen would make just ninety cents per day, a wage no one could live on.

Train crews working for the Baltimore & Ohio earned the second-lowest pay in the industry, the only major road paying less being the New York Central. Firemen on the Baltimore & Ohio went from earning $55.00 a month in 1873 to $30.00 and conductors from $90.00 to $30.00, the same as they'd made in 1842. In 1876, first-class firemen and brakemen made $1.50 per trip and second-class ones $1.35. Out of this, they had to pay out of their own pockets for stays in hotels and to travel back home after reaching their destinations.

The Baltimore & Ohio was the first railroad company in the United States. It was founded by Baltimore businessmen concerned that the city's port was losing business because no canals connected it inland and the existing highway system wasn't up to the task of moving all the goods that could be brought or sent overseas by ships. In 1825, Baltimore bankers Philip E. Thomas and George Brown thought their city would be best served by a "rail road" of the sort then in use in England that would connect the city to the Ohio River. Railroad tracks offered a more efficient way of moving goods because they eliminated issues such as muddy or pothole-laden roads. The Maryland legislature incorporated the Baltimore & Ohio Railroad on February 28, 1827.

It would have two lines, one going to the Potomac River and the other to the Ohio River. The stone blocks used for the road's bed were first laid on July 4, 1830. Its first section connected Ellicott's Mills to Baltimore, a stretch of thirteen miles, and its first train ran on January 7, 1830. In the early days, trains were pulled by teams of horses changed every six or seven miles, but they weren't capable of efficiently moving freights the required distances. For this, the Baltimore & Ohio needed a machine.

Its first test for this idea was done by Peter Cooper's steam engine *Tom Thumb* in August 1830. It made the trip from Baltimore to Ellicott's Mills and back with speeds up to eighteen miles per hour while pushing a carriage with eighteen passengers. Considered a success, it couldn't be used for regular work because it was experimental.

To entice someone to build an engine that could do the job, the Baltimore & Ohio set up a contest to produce a locomotive suitable for its needs. The first prize paid $4,000 and the second $3,500. A winning machine could weigh no more than three and one-half tons and be capable of going a sustained fifteen miles per hour while pulling fifteen tons. Only four entries were submitted. The road adopted the *York*, an eight-wheel engine that could do thirty miles per hour on a straightway and fifteen around curves.

The Baltimore & Ohio's tracks initially terminated at Wheeling, Virginia (now West Virginia). From there, cars had to be ferried across the river to the Central Ohio Railroad. The Baltimore & Ohio's directors realized Wheeling wasn't going to be sufficient for their ambitions to expand westward, so they had tracks built to Parkersburg, Virginia (now West Virginia). From there,

"Peter Cooper's Tom Thumb." Bureau of Public Roads, Department of Commerce, circa 1900–50. *Library of Congress Prints and Photographs.*

cars were ferried across the Ohio River to Cincinnati, where two other railroads, the Marietta & Cincinnati and the Ohio & Mississippi, took them farther west. Garrett decided to build bridges to connect Parkersburg and Wheeling directly to Ohio rather than relying on ferries. The Baltimore & Ohio bought the Central Ohio in 1869, allowing it to reach Sandusky and thus give it access to the Great Lakes.

When hard economic times came, the pain of belt tightening was felt primarily by the road's employees. Garrett and his fellow officers saw workers as nothing more than disposable commodities, so they couldn't care less if the wage cut on July 16 resulted in their men starving. Never in his life had Garrett faced hardship. He was born into a wealthy Baltimore family on July 31, 1820, and for a time worked for his father's company, Robert Garrett & Sons. He also invested in Baltimore real estate and in stocks that included the Baltimore & Ohio. As one of its major stockholders, in 1856 he became concerned about the road's mismanagement, believing political influence was causing its ills. He became one of its directors in October 1857 and its president the next year. A notorious penny-pincher, he capped his annual salary to $4,000 and that of the road's vice presidents to $6,000.

On the day of the Baltimore & Ohio's latest wage reduction, thirty-two firemen left their trains at Baltimore's Camden Station, with others

John W. Garrett. Bain News Service, date unknown. *Library of Congress Prints and Photographs.*

following suit. The road replaced them with strike-breakers. Baltimore's mayor ordered the police to arrest three strikers for causing a "riot." According to Philip S. Foner's *The Great Labor Uprising of 1877*, the next day, thirty-eight "engineers joined with the striking firemen, and that evening 140 members of the Baltimore Boxes and Sawyer's Union and 800 tin can makers" united with them because of their own low wages. Despite this, trains never stopped.

This was unfortunate for the Baltimore & Ohio because it allowed discontented workers to travel to Martinsburg, West Virginia, to cause the trouble there. A city six hours away from Baltimore with about seven thousand inhabitants, Martinsburg served as a major relay station in the line where the train crews switched out. It was a major chokepoint because all trains coming out of Baltimore had to pass through here to continue west. Men from Baltimore stirred up their Martinsburg brethren, and by evening of the sixteenth, the firemen had struck. Many of them were members of the recently formed Trainmen's Union (see chapter 6), which had started on one of the Pennsylvania Railroad's subsidiaries, the Pittsburgh, Fort Wayne & Chicago.

The strikers stopped all freight trains from moving through the city, parking uncoupled engines in the roundhouse. Martinsburg's mayor, A.P. Shutt, owned the city's main hotel, Berkeley House. It was in his best interest to get the trains moving again to avoid a dip in business, so he spoke to the striking men. This only upset them. They told him that no trains would run until their wages were restored. He tried to have the strike's leaders arrested, but no one would do it. Undaunted, he brought in a group of men to get the trains started, but the strikers prevented them from doing so. The next day, the engineers joined the strike.

The stoppage prevented all trains from heading any farther west, keeping them from entering Ohio and its vast network there. Shutt notified Baltimore & Ohio officials of the work stoppage, prompting one of its two vice presidents, John King Jr., to contact West Virginia's governor, Henry M. Mathews, and inform him there was a riot in Martinsburg that the local police couldn't put down. Not bothering to determine if there really was one going on (there wasn't), Mathews decided to send out the state militia to deal with it, such as it was. Two years earlier, the state militia had been made into a poorly trained all-volunteer force consisting of just four companies. Mathews sent a telegraph to state militia colonel C.J. Faulkner, head of the Berkeley Light Infantry, to get the trains running. Among the militia's ranks were many railroaders.

On July 17 at around eight o'clock in the morning, men from the Berkeley Light Infantry climbed on board a train headed out of the depot. One of the strikers, William Vandergriff, threw a switch with the intention of knocking the train off the track. Private John Poisal, a railroader in his civilian life, leaped off the car and moved the switch back.

The armed Vandergriff fired his pistol at Poisal, and the bullet grazed his head. Poisal shot back, hitting Vandergriff in the hips. Other strikers opened up on Poisal. Bullets struck his left arm and right hand. Despite this, the militia was disinclined to fire on fellow railroad workers, forcing crew to abandon the train. Vandergriff succumbed to his wounds on July 28 and was buried in Green Hill Cemetery. This was the first violence of the strike, one that would soon expand to other parts of the United States.

Strikers from other locations made their way to the city, swelling their numbers to eight hundred by July 18. Faulkner hadn't ordered anyone to fire on the strikers and wanted no violence, so he sent a telegraph to the governor informing him that he could do no more. The Berkley Light Infantry was ordered home. The governor ordered the Wheeling-based Mathews Light Guard to Martinsburg. Commanded by Colonel R.L. Delaplaine, it arrived at 7:30 a.m. on July 18. Delaplaine's troops kept the peace, but no freight trains moved. He reported to the governor that the entire town would rise up with the strikers if violence broke out.

A day earlier, Garrett had telegraphed President Rutherford B. Hayes requesting federal troops be sent to Martinsburg. He stated that he wouldn't mind if federal troops did whatever was necessary to get his trains running. Hayes had no interest in doing the bidding of the railroads, but the next day, Governor Mathews also asked him for troops. Hayes demanded more information. Mathews replied that he had only forty reliable men and it would take up to ten days to form a new company, during which time the strikers may well destroy property and lives could be lost.

Although Hayes sympathized with the workers and disliked railroads and all their machinations such as watering down stock and giving secret rebates, he didn't think it was right for men to keep others from working. He was also a keen protector of private property, but he wouldn't send troops anywhere

Strike in Martinsburg. Illustrated by Fred B. Schell, from *Harper's Weekly*, August 11, 1877. *Library of Congress Prints and Photographs.*

110
B&O.R.R

Above left: President Rutherford B. Hayes. Painted by G.F. Gilman, 1877. *Library of Congress Prints and Photographs.*

Above right: George Washington McCrary, circa 1860–70. *Library of Congress Prints and Photographs.*

Left: Major General Winfield Scott Hancock during the Civil War. Brady's National Photographic Portrait Galleries. *Library of Congress Prints and Photographs.*

without knowing what was going on. It wasn't until he learned that lives had been lost and property damaged that he acquiesced.

He told Secretary of War George W. McCrary to send troops. McCrary, in turn, ordered Major General Winfield Scott Hancock, commander of the Military Division of the Atlantic, to allocate the needed men. A total of three hundred from Fort McHenry and Washington Arsenal headed to

Martinsburg. Under the command of breveted Major General William H. French, the force arrived on the morning of July 19. The strikers didn't attempt to stop them. By this point there were over 100 engines and about 1,500 freight cars standing idle, blocking all railroad entrances into town, although passenger and mail trains continued to pass through.

At ten o'clock that morning, a crew boarded a train and drove it west for about a mile until reaching the strikers' headquarters. Intimidated by the gathered strikers, the crew detrained and made themselves scarce. A second crew arrived accompanied by federal soldiers. George Zepp, whose brother Dick was one of the strike's leaders, decided to serve as the fireman for the train despite pleas from his mother and sisters to turn back. When strikers tried to stop him from boarding, he drew a revolver to drive them off and then climbed on board. The train headed out.

At around three o'clock in the afternoon, William N. Clements, general agent of the road at Locust Point in Baltimore, climbed on board a train to serve as its engineer. As it moved out of a siding, armed strikers attempted to stop it, warning Clements that they'd shoot him if he didn't halt. He ignored them. They followed the train as it slowly gathered speed with the intent of stopping it, but when federal troops came at them with fixed bayonets, they broke and ran. Trains moved freely in and out of town by July 20. Those heading west wouldn't get past Cincinnati, where more strikes had erupted.

CHAPTER 5
RAILROADED BY STANDARD OIL

If mapped out, the history of nearly every railroad to operate in the United States looks like a backward family tree. At the top are a number of unrelated railroads that slowly merged or bought one another until they became behemoths with names unrelated to their beginnings, such as CSX or Norfolk Southern. The Pennsylvania Railroad, often referred to as the Pennsy, is different. The core company along with its name ran continuously from its start in 1846 to its merger with New York Central in 1968. West of Pittsburgh, the Pennsy owned a number of subsidiary roads that ran under their own names but were controlled by the Pennsy's president and its officers.

The Pennsy had its origin in the 1830s. At that time, the Commonwealth of Pennsylvania ran the State Works System to move goods to and from Philadelphia to the Ohio River. It consisted of a series of short-line railroads and canals that made it inefficient and unable to complete with the Erie Canal in New York or the Baltimore & Ohio Railroad in Maryland. This reduced Philadelphia's commercial significance, prompting local businessmen to advocate for the creation a single railroad to connect Philadelphia to the Ohio River.

Economic conditions weren't right to start this venture until 1846. On April 13 of that year, the Pennsylvania legislature approved a charter for the Pennsylvania Railroad. Another bill allowed the Baltimore & Ohio to connect to Pittsburgh on April 21 only if the Pennsy didn't meet the terms of its charter, which stipulated that it have under contract at least thirty miles of track plus $3 million in pledged subscriptions, $1 million of which had to be collected by July 30, 1847. The Pennsy met all the conditions, keeping the Baltimore & Ohio out of Pittsburgh for the time being.

Thomas A. Scott. Illustration by Frederick Gutekunst, 1873. *Library of Congress Prints and Photographs.*

Opening on September 1, 1849, the Pennsy's first section connected Lewistown to Harrisburg. In 1857, it bought the ailing State Works System. In exchange, it was made exempt from freight tonnage taxes in perpetuity. The first Pennsy train to travel uninterrupted from Philadelphia to Pittsburgh did so on December 10, 1852, but not exclusively on its own tracks. That milestone wouldn't happen until June 27, 1858.

Another significant event in the company's history occurred in 1850, when the Pennsy's chief engineer, John Edgar Thomson, hired Thomas Alexander Scott to become the stationmaster for Duncansville. No one knew it at the time, but Scott would one day become one of the road's most important presidents. Born in his family's hotel in Fort Loudon, Pennsylvania, on December 28, 1824, Scott's first job was as a clerk for his brother-in-law James Patton, the collector of tolls in Columbia, Pennsylvania. Scott left this position to run a small sawmill in town, which secured a contract from the state to provide lumber for the construction of bridges. It did well until a flood destroyed it. Scott's next venture, an icehouse, failed.

He became the Pennsy's first vice president in 1860. The next year, he left the road to join the Union army, which put him in charge of all Union telegraph lines and railroads. He took control of the railroads and placed Thomas T. Eckert, Western Union's general manager, in charge of the telegraphs. Scott later became an assistant to the secretary of war.

Resigning from the army on June 1, 1862, Scott returned to the Pennsy as a vice president. That September, he personally took a train to Antietam to deliver desperately needed ammunition to the battle going on there. A year later, he returned to the army, this time serving as a colonel on General Joseph Hooker's staff as the assistant quartermaster. When Hooker needed reinforcements in Chattanooga, Scott rushed them from Louisville, Kentucky, to Nashville via the railroad.

Scott became the Pennsy's president on May 27, 1874. Although the economy was dire, his road was the largest single system in the world, making him one of the most powerful men in the United States who regularly who got his way. That is, until an upstart petroleum refiner in Ohio named Standard Oil put him in his place.

Standard's chief product was kerosene, a product so popular in America that twenty million gallons of it were used in 1880 alone. Millions more were exported to Asia. Kerosene was first extracted from coal in 1846 by Abraham Gesner of Canada. It could also be extracted from crude oil, and in 1859, a British immigrant living in Cleveland, Samuel Andrews, figured a way to refine more petroleum out of a barrel of crude than before, increasing its output significantly. In 1863, he established his own refinery, Andrews, Clark & Company, with some of its financing coming from Maurice B. Clark and John D. Rockefeller.

Rockefeller was born in Richford, New York, on July 8, 1839. His family moved to Ohio, settling first in Strongsville and then relocating in 1853 to Parma, where Rockefeller came of age. His father, a traveling businessman, was gone for long periods, leaving young John to become especially close to his mother, a fervent Baptist. He started his first job as a bookkeeper and clerk in September 1855 at Issac L. Hewitt and Henry B. Tuttle, a company that bought and sold produce for others on commission. He left in the spring of 1859 to set up his own commission house with partner Clark that dealt in, among other things, agricultural products.

The company often bought grain from Henry M. Flagler, who at the time lived in and operated out of Bellevue, Ohio. Born in the small New York town of Hopewell, one of Flagler's earliest jobs was as a clerk working in a store in the village of Republic, Ohio, where he sold shoes, candles, and soap. Although he made just five dollars a month, he saved enough to become a grain dealer in Bellevue. He made a small fortune distilling liquor and then lost it in the salt business. Moving to Cleveland, he became a partner in a distillery with Rockefeller and Andrews.

In 1865, Andrews and Rockefeller formed a new company, Rockefeller & Andrews, whose purpose was to refine crude oil into kerosene. Why choose oil refining despite the fact that Cleveland was two hundred miles from the Pennsylvania oil fields? It was connected to the big railroads and was a major Lake Erie port from which oil products could be sent to New York City. Andrews took charge of production, Rockefeller of the business. In an era when most bosses were tyrants, Andrews became known for his kindness and rarely admonished his men.

An elderly John D. Rockefeller stands alongside his bicycle in 1913. *Library of Congress Prints and Photographs.*

To grow the business, Rockefeller began combining with other Cleveland refiners. He incorporated this growing conglomerate as Standard Oil on January 10, 1870. In addition to Andrews and his brother, Rockefeller brought in Flagler as a partner, a man who drove some of the hardest bargains the company would make in its first decade. It would, for example, use the chaos of the Panic of 1873 to buy many small refiners, and the

John D. Rockefeller's opulent Cleveland house burned down on December 17, 1917. Image from a postcard printed by F.M. Kirby & Co., circa 1907–15. *Author's collection.*

next year, its control of oil refining was so great it was able to reduce the production of kerosene enough to drive the price up.

The trouble oil refiners had at this time was that many of the foreign nations buying oil from the United States only wanted crude because they could refine and sell it at a lower price domestically. France put a tariff on American refined oil to support its own refineries. Some of Pennsylvania's refiners hatched a secret plan to do something about this. They would keep prices high by reducing output, giving refiners the ability to dictate the price per barrel on crude. With the market cornered, they'd use their power to convince railroads to stop shipping crude altogether and to move their refined oil at a lower price than regular customers received. The new venture, called the South Improvement Company, was incorporated by the Pennsylvania legislature on May 1, 1871.

At first Rockefeller and Flagler didn't think much of the plan, but once they decided to join, Standard's stockholders bought most of the new venture's shares. A contract between Standard and several railroads was drawn up stipulating that 45 percent of oil would be shipped on the Pennsylvania and Baltimore & Ohio Railroads, and the rest would be divided between the New York Central and Erie Railroads.

Standard Oil's refinery in Cleveland, 1896. *Library of Congress Prints and Photographs.*

The railroads had to provide a sufficient number of storage tanks to hold the oil at both the onboarding and offloading ends. They also had the right to replace South Improvement's business if a competitor offered the same amount or more business. The railroads involved would give rebates on crude or refined oil back to South Improvement. Rebates worked like this. South Improvement refiners would, as an example, pay the full list price of two dollars per gross for shipping their product from Cleveland to New York City or Pittsburgh to New York City. The roads would then return fifty cents per gross back to South Improvement after shipment. This was done secretly to prevent others who were shipping freight on the roads from complaining or demanding similar rates.

Rockefeller used South Improvement as an excuse to bully other Cleveland refiners to sell out to his company. In three months' time, about twenty-one of the twenty-six refineries in the city agreed, increasing Standard's capacity from about 1,500 to 10,000 barrels a day. Standard also made a secret deal via a shell company with the Pennsy that dictated that it would receive a rebate of one dollar for each barrel it shipped and one dollar for each barrel its competitors shipped!

After learning the sordid details of this deal, the Pennsylvania legislature rescinded South Improvement's charter before its contracts went into effect. With that venture dead, the railroads agreed to establish a group rate, usually between seventy-five and eighty cents per barrel, that would be the same no matter the distance.

Flagler was Standard's primary negotiator, and he drove a hard bargain. His company received its rebates and demanded that the railroads it used refuse to ship refined oil from competitors. Rockefeller made sure deals weren't written down because public exposure of a paper trail was what had ended the South Improvement Company. Standard strong-armed the railroads into these agreements by threatening to ship all their products using ships on Lake Erie if it didn't get its way. As a result of all its maneuvers, Standard controlled about 90 percent of the oil business in the United States by 1878, something not generally known until *The Atlantic* published "The Story of a Great Monopoly" in its March 1881 issue.

Standard's control worried the large railroads because it meant this upstart oil refiner could completely eliminate nearly all petroleum shipping on a given line if it didn't meet Standard's demands. In 1876, the Empire Transportation Company, in which the Pennsy had a stake, decided to challenge Standard's monopoly. Empire's president, Joseph D. Potts, was born on December 4, 1829, in Springton Forge, Pennsylvania. He began his railroad career in 1852 with the Sunbury & Erie Railroad, which became the Philadelphia & Erie Railroad. When the Pennsy took it over in 1862, he became its general manager. He took charge of Empire in 1865.

Empire owned 4,500 railroad cars and operated eighteen steam liners and sailing ships on the Great Lakes, giving it access to 33 percent of railroads in the nation. In Erie, Pennsylvania, it had two grain elevators and ample docks. One of its specialties was the transportation of mineral oil via its four hundred miles of pipelines. Potts, with the full support of the Pennsy, thought Empire could challenge Standard by building a refinery at the Bradford oil field, to which Empire was already connected.

The Bradford field covered about eighty-four thousand acres spanning parts of the Pennsylvania–New York border. The Foster Oil Company was the first to tap into it in 1871. At first it seemed a bust because the crude extracted was mixed with sand that clogged the machinery, but in 1875, the Crocker well showed if you went deep enough, it paid well. The Bradford oil field produced about 90 percent of the United States' crude oil by 1881.

Standard didn't like what it considered poaching on its business one bit. Even more galling, Empire and the Pennsy refused to give it the same rates it received on the New York Central and Erie Railroads. Of the Pennsy's oil traffic, 65 percent was from Standard, so when, in 1877 Rockefeller threatened to withdraw all of Standard's business if Empire didn't get out of the refinery business, the Pennsy pressured Potts to sell Empire's refineries. He refused.

Rockefeller went to war. He ordered the increased production of refined oil and then sold it for less than what Empire did. He convinced the Erie

This photo of Bradford, Pennsylvania, was taken from Harrisburg Hill. West & Waddell, circa 1875. *Library of Congress Prints and Photographs.*

Oil Exchange in Bradford, Pennsylvania. West & Waddell, circa 1860–90. *Library of Congress Prints and Photographs.*

and New York Central Railroads to give him even lower rates and then stopped shipping all of Standard's products on the Pennsy. This reduction of business prompted Scott to take drastic measures. Although his road didn't own Empire wholly, it had the option to buy its remaining shares, so it did. Scott sold all of Empire's assets to Standard and then made up with Rockefeller, regaining much of his road's lost business. Still, the hit to the Pennsy's bottom line was significant, and he had to make it up somewhere. He set his sights on his workforce.

CHAPTER 6

STRIKE ON THE PENNSYLVANIA RAILROAD

All Pennsylvania Railroad coal trains were doubleheaders by the late spring of 1877. On June 1, a 10 percent wage cut was implemented. Although the Pennsy's revenues since 1877 had dropped from an average of $7 million to $4.5 million a year, the amount of freight it hauled had increased. Had it wanted to, it could have afforded to do better than paying some of its workers just seventy-five cents a day.

Wanting no additional doubleheaders and angered by the wage cut, railroad workers secretly assembled on June 2 at Dietrich's Hall in Pennsylvania's Allegheny City (now part of Pittsburgh) to discuss what they could do. They formed the Trainmen's Union, which differed from the exclusive one the engineers had by accepting all train crew members no matter what their skill level. Members vowed to walk off the job if railroads implemented any more wage cuts or increased the use of doubleheaders.

The union elected Robert Ammon as its head and sent him out to organize lodges where he could, paying all his travel expenses. Of Prussian descent, Ammon was born in New Jersey on June 9, 1852, but was raised in Pittsburgh, where his father worked as a successful insurance executive. After the strike, Allan Pinkerton, the man who started the famous detective agency bearing his name, investigated Ammon. Many of the more salacious parts of the latter's life story come from Pinkerton's brief biography, which has to be treated with suspicion because the detective despised Ammon.

At the age of sixteen, Ammon was expelled from Capital University in Columbus, Ohio, for his unruliness alongside the son of a railroad executive.

Robert Ammon sending a telegraph. Illustration by John Donaghy. From *Frank Leslie's Illustrated Newspaper*, August 11, 1877. *Library of Congress Prints and Photographs.*

He served in the U.S. Army for a time as a bugler and traveled abroad in South America and China. Returning to the United States, he became a representative for four insurance agencies in Chicago before moving to Collinwood, Ohio, where he was proprietor of a hotel for nearly two years. This venture ended when it burned down. Pinkerton implied the fire was not accidental.

Ammon returned to Pittsburgh in the summer of 1876 with his wife (Pinkerton claimed they weren't yet married) and first child. With him, Ammon brought a letter of introduction to J.D. Layng, the general manager of the Pittsburgh, Fort Wayne & Chicago Railroad, a subsidiary of the Pennsy. He was hired on as a brakeman. From his work in insurance, Ammon had an income of forty dollars a month in addition to what he earned as a railroad crewman.

Departing for his Trainmen's Union recruitment effort on June 4, Ammon spent the next weeks traveling far and wide. One lodge he organized was in Martinsburg, West Virginia, about which he later recalled, "They talked most loud at Martinsburg, but I thought it was all wind. I didn't think they would strike at all." And: "I was acquainted with the men down there, and didn't think it amounted to a row of pins."

Spies infiltrated the Trainmen's Union and reported the names of those involved to the Pennsy. As a result, Ammon was fired on June 24. Shortly after his separation from the Pittsburgh, Fort Wayne & Chicago, the weakened union faced the crisis it had anticipated. The Pennsy announced that freight trains going east from Pittsburgh to Altoona, a distance of 116 miles, would be doubleheaders. Previously, trains traveled as far as Derry, which was forty-eight miles from Pittsburgh. The increased length and time of the trip earned crews not a penny more. Running trains twice the length with the same number of men allowed the Pennsy to dismiss nearly half its freight crews.

On the morning of July 19, a crew in Pittsburgh told the dispatcher that they wouldn't take their train out. The dispatcher failed to find replacements. The strikers threw stones at the crew of another train trying to leave, making it stop. More joined them. They headed to the East Liberty Stockyards, where yard men were recruited. Not a single freight train departed after this first act of defiance, although the strikers allowed passenger and mail trains to pass, the latter because stopping one of those would result in federal troops being deployed.

That night, union members met at Phoenix Hall on Eleventh Street, where they decided to continue the strike and drew up a list of demands. These included the restoration of wages, rehiring workers fired for taking

The Sourbeck House in Alliance, Ohio, served as a Pittsburgh, Wayne & Chicago Railroad station. Lithograph by Augustus Hani, circa 1864–69. *Library of Congress Prints and Photographs.*

part in the strike, the abolishment of doubleheaders save for coal trains, and that all engines would have their own fireman. Many of Pittsburgh's trade unions offered their support. Citizens of western Pennsylvania on the whole sympathized with the strikers because they well knew how terribly the Pennsy treated its workers.

Ammon was working in the Pennsylvania oil fields when the strike broke out. While in Parker, he received a telegram on July 18 from a friend telling him that trouble was expected in Pittsburgh. The friend asked if he would come. Ammon ignored it, but upon receiving a second telegram that night urging him to reconsider, he took a train there, arriving on the morning of the nineteenth. He was met by friends, all of whom were conductors and brakemen working for the Pennsy or one of its subsidiaries. They urged him to participate in the coming strike. He refused to go with them to the superintendent's office because he no longer worked for the company.

That same day, he went to Allegheny City, where he had a house. After having breakfast and playing with his baby, he went to sleep. Men from the Pittsburgh, Fort Wayne & Chicago knocked on the door asking for him. His wife turned them away, as Ammon was asleep. They soon returned. Hearing them, Ammon came downstairs and asked them what they wanted. They implored that he join the strike. He declined, considering them "scabs." Later, two conductors and five brakemen he knew stopped by and asked him to come. He relented. He was, after all, still head of the Trainmen's Union. On June 22, he took control of the Pittsburgh, Fort Wayne & Chicago Railroad's dispatcher's office in Allegheny City and for three days oversaw passenger traffic.

Pennsylvania Governor John F. Hartranft issued a proclamation that the strikers had to disperse. It was up to Allegheny County's sheriff, Richard H. Fife, to enforce it. He went to the Pennsy's Pittsburgh yards, climbed on top of a locomotive, told the men they needed to desist from interfering with the running of trains, and then read the governor's proclamation. Just as he readied to get down, someone in the crowd shouted, "Give us a loaf of bread." Another suggested the sheriff bring them a carload of bread, which resulted in laughter and cheering. The sheriff telegraphed the governor that the strikers had refused the order.

The governor called out the state militia stationed in Pittsburgh. It either wouldn't or couldn't control the strikers, so he ordered the First Division of Philadelphia consisting of 1,800 men under the command of Major General Robert M. Brinton to deal with the strike in Pittsburgh. Brinton had fought in the Civil War and was thirty-five at the time of his trip to

This illustration of Pennsylvania Governor John F. Hartranft by Frenzeny and Tavernier is based on a photograph by F. Gutekunst. From *Harper's Weekly*, November 27, 1875. *Library of Congress Prints and Photographs.*

Pittsburgh. His division consisted of infantry, cavalry (the Black Hussars), and two Gatling guns. A train carried the division and its equipment to Pittsburgh. Arriving at three o'clock in the afternoon of July 22, the division detrained and at 3:40 p.m. headed for the Twenty-Eighth Street railroad crossing, where strikers had assembled to block trains. Here a "mob"—consisting mostly of onlookers rather than anyone keen on making trouble—had gathered. One estimate put its number at five thousand. The First Division was supported by the Pittsburgh-based Sixth Division, commanded by Major General Alfred L. Pearson, who was the highest-ranking officer in the city.

Led by Sheriff Fife and fifteen of his deputies, the soldiers marched to Twenty-Eighth Street. Fife had with him fifteen arrest warrants. He tried to apprehend the ringleader, but this fellow waved a bat and told his followers to "give them hell." Some of the strikers tried to wrestle rifles from the soldiers, and they responded with bayonet thrusts, one of which resulted in a wound. The Black Hussars dismounted to clear the crowd. They were met with a shower of rocks from the hills above and a few shots from revolvers.

Without an order to do so, the First Division fired above the heads of the crowd, but the rocks continued to fly. The soldiers fired again, this time into the crowd, killing fourteen to sixteen and wounding somewhere between thirty-six and forty, many of whom were women and children. Disgusted, members of Pittsburgh's Fourteenth and Eighteenth Regiments threw down their weapons, which the crowd appropriated. Hutchinson's Battery declined to join them.

This act of violence enraged many in Pittsburgh, so what started as a crowd of mostly spectators turned into a mob wanting revenge. Two gun factories—Johnson's on Smithfield Street and Brown's on Wood Street—were gutted, as were the city's gun stores. Members of the mob also looted tobacco and liquor stores. One eyewitness, fifteen-year-old Helen Crombie, observed that "plenty of people [were] drunk." Afterward, about three thousand armed men headed down Fifth Avenue playing drums and carrying flags. The remaining soldiers retreated to the Pennsy's Twenty-Sixth Street roundhouse at six o'clock that evening.

Two hours later, about one thousand men surrounded the militia's makeshift fortress, bringing with them a piece of artillery left behind by Hutchinson's Battery. It was never fired. Seven men tried to work it, and each time they were shot by Sergeant Harvey Johnson and two other soldiers. The militia's return fire was in any case too heavy for the attackers to enter the roundhouse. Bystanders died during the exchange of fire, including, the *St. Louis Globe-Democrat* reported, "a woman sitting on her door-step [who] was shot and died instantly." Sometime during the night, Sheriff Fife also lost his life. The mob dispersed when rumors spread that Gatling guns were being readied.

The reprieve didn't last long. Sometime after eleven o'clock that evening, about four thousand well-armed men split into two columns, one heading up Pennsylvania Avenue and the other Liberty Avenue, at which about thirty thousand people assembled. Idle freight cars along the many sidings containing merchandise, grain, produce, coke, cake, and oil were looted or set afire. Strikers seized a coke car from the Allegheny Valley Railroad, poured petroleum onto it, and lit it up. At around 6:30 the next morning, they pushed it onto the Pennsy's tracks and sent it into the roundhouse, setting it ablaze and forcing the soldiers within to abandon their shelter.

The First Division made its way to the federally controlled Allegheny Arsenal hoping for refuge. This they were refused on the grounds that they would bring the whole mob on the place, although the division's wounded were taken in. From there the militia headed down Butler Street, with a mob of about one thousand on their heels. During the retreat, five soldiers died and at least eleven were wounded. The militia crossed the Allegheny River via the Sharpsburg Bridge. With the mob still in pursuit, the division split into small detachments, forcing its pursuers to divide as well. The First Division made it out of the city and to the safety of the Allegheny County Workhouse about ten miles way.

The mob inflicted between $8 and $10 million worth of damage on Pennsylvania Railroad property. It spent its remaining energy destroying property and offices belonging to the Panhandle Railroad; the Pullman Company; the Cleveland, Cincinnati, Chicago & St. Louis Railroad; and the Adams Express Company. Union Station and Union Hotel burned as well. The last major structure engulfed by flames was a large grain elevator on the corner of Washington and Liberty Streets. Fires destroyed over one hundred

"Burning of the Round-house at Pittsburgh." From *Harper's Weekly*, August 11, 1877. *Library of Congress Prints and Photographs.*

Entrance to the Allegheny Arsenal. Detroit Publishing Co., circa 1900–15. *Library of Congress Prints and Photographs.*

"Destruction of the Union Depot and Hotel at Pittsburgh." Illustration by F.B. Schell. From *Frank Leslie's Illustrated Newspaper*, 1877. *Library of Congress Prints and Photographs.*

locomotives and two thousand railroad cars. The police took control of the city after the rioters tired themselves out.

Ammon watched these events from his house, which stood high enough on a hill for him to see using a spyglass. He said had he been there, he'd have tried to stop the destruction of property, and possibly succeeded. When asked at a hearing convened by Pennsylvania lawmakers why people stood by and did nothing about it, Ammon said he believed it was because they hated the Pennsy. It had driven many local businesses to close since its arrival in the city.

Pennsy President Thomas Alexander Scott wanted the federal government to intervene, but President Rutherford Hayes wouldn't send federal troops to Pennsylvania unless Governor Hartranft requested them, and Hartranft was out west on a trip financed by Scott. After the governor arrived home and made the request, Hayes sent fifty men from Columbus, Ohio, to Pittsburgh to guard the Allegheny Arsenal. Scott wanted Hayes to break the strike by using federal troops to run the trains, but he refused to intervene.

Governor Hartranft arrived in Pittsburgh on July 25. Pinkerton claims that Ammon stopped the governor's train. In his book *Strikers, Communists, Tramps and Detectives*, Pinkerton wrote that Ammon "*forced* [his emphasis] the

Chief Executive of…Pennsylvania to the platform, where amid the wild yells of the thousands who had by this time gathered about, he [Ammon] stammered out a few words which might be taken to mean very much or very little. Then the Governor was permitted to retire." More sober sources say Ammon helped the governor get into Pittsburgh.

The strike continued. On the twenty-sixth, Ammon suggested that the men of the Pittsburgh, Fort Wayne & Chicago Railroad give up the strike. This got him nothing but jeers and hisses, so he resigned. Once again Pinkerton has an alternative version of this event. In his telling, Ammon was forced out because the more conservative members of the Trainmen's Union felt he'd gone too far boarding Governor Hartranft's train car.

Ammon was arrested on July 30 by W.D. Ross, chief of Allegheny City's police, and briefly put in jail, but his case never went to trial. General Pearson was charged with murder, but a grand jury declined to indict him because no witnesses could be found swearing that he gave the order for his troops to fire. Courts also litigated who would pay for the damages and ultimately held Allegheny County liable.

CHAPTER 7

THE STRIKE SPREADS TO OHIO

As word of the strike traveled along railroad lines, it most likely reached Cleveland and its surrounding towns and villages via the Cleveland & Pittsburgh Railroad, which the Pennsy had leased in 1871 for ninety-nine years. Word of the strike galvanized men on other railroads to implement work stoppages. One of those was the Lake Shore & Southern Michigan, a feeder road for the New York Central.

The Lake Shore, which connected Buffalo to Chicago, got its name because its main line hugged the southern shore of Lake Erie from one end to the other. Made up of eight former roads that had merged over the years, the Lake Shore proper began on August 10, 1869, and branch lines were later added. It also controlled other roads that still ran under their own names. Between 1870 and the beginning of 1874, it aggressively expanded, spending almost $2.5 million for this effort. The Panic of 1873 put an abrupt stop to that.

The road's president was William H. Vanderbilt, the eldest son of Cornelius Vanderbilt, known during his lifetime as the "Commodore" because he'd made his fortune in the steamship and shipping businesses. In the 1850s, Cornelius began investing in railroads, and by the time of his death on January 4, 1877, he oversaw the New York Central.

When it came time for Cornelius to send William to school, he hadn't yet made his fortune, so he placed him at the modest Columbia Grammar School. The elder Vanderbilt didn't think much of his son and for many years belittled him, never supporting him in any of his ventures. Despite

William H. Vanderbilt, circa 1870–71. *Library of Congress Prints and Photographs.*

this, William repeatedly proved himself capable of doing anything he set his mind to, and in time, he and his father reconciled. This lack of parental support humbled the younger Vanderbilt in a way that made his attitude toward those who worked for him much different than his fellow railroad presidents such as Thomas Scott or John Garrett.

William made the first two railroads he was put in charge of quite profitable, and he was instrumental in growing the New York Central into the powerhouse it became. In addition to being head of this road and the Lake Shore, he was president of the Michigan Central Railroad. He also oversaw several telegraph, telephone, and electric light companies. By the time of his death in 1883, it's said he was the richest man in the world. He was worth $194,000, about $200 million today. He was known as the "Colossus of Roads."

The Lake Shore strike began on July 22 at three o'clock in the afternoon at Collinwood, a village east of Cleveland that has since become one of that city's neighborhoods. Brakemen and firemen walked off the job, and the engineers refused to run trains without experienced crewmen. The strike spread into Cleveland, where the local militia, the Grays, kept watch for trouble but found none.

The next day, about two hundred to three hundred workers met in Collinwood to discuss their demands, which included the abolition of different classes of engineers, an increase in wages for engineers to $3.50 and firemen to $1.75 for a run of one hundred miles or less, and that brakemen and firemen would be issued monthly passes for their divisions so they wouldn't have to pay for the trip home after a run. All men would be paid overtime if detained over ten hours on the Erie Division and twelve hours on the Toledo. They further demanded that the recent 10 percent pay cut be restored, that no one who struck should be fired, and that they be paid on the fifteenth of every month.

The men gave their demands to road superintendent Charles Paine, who lived in Cleveland. Born in New Hampshire in 1830, he was a lifelong railroad man. He began his career at the age of fifteen with the Central Vermont Railroad and became the Lake Shore's superintendent in 1872, a position he'd keep for the next twenty-three years. He promised to forward the strikers' demands to Vanderbilt. In return, the men pledged not to destroy any company property.

The day after the Lake Shore men issued their demands, a *Cleveland Plain Dealer* reporter drove to Collinwood to check out the conditions. To his surprise, all was quiet. He couldn't find anyone out and about to interview, so he finally went into a real estate office to find someone to speak with. There, a person suggested that the strikers might be at the roundhouse, where he found a dozen firemen and brakemen. They told him they couldn't make a living on their current wages. One man said when he took an engine into Cleveland, he had to pay a twenty-five-cent fare to get back home. The strikers planned to remain peaceful. They'd forced the saloons to shut down because they didn't want their fellow workers to get drunk and do something stupid.

Closing the saloons was a wise decision. In places where strikers did get liquored up, things could get out of control. This happened in Wapakoneta, Ohio, where workers building the Scioto Valley Railroad walked off the job because of a disagreement over pay. When told by a hotel proprietor that they'd had enough to drink, they trashed his place and then departed and caused trouble elsewhere in the village. Unable to control the rioters, the Auglaize County sheriff sent for the Chapman Guards from Piketon to restore order and arrest the ringleaders, which they did.

The reason Collinwood strikers were adamantly against violence was to avoid what had happened at Standard Oil earlier that year. On the morning of April 19, coopers learned that their wages would be reduced by 10 percent. This, they contended, would leave them destitute, so they struck. Standard Oil insisted the cut was necessary. The depression had affected sales, so the company needed to lower wages to break even.

Most of the coopers came from the kingdom of Bohemia, which is now (mostly) the Czech Republic. After walking off the job, they headed to offices of the Czech-language socialist newspaper *Dělnické Listy* (*Workingmen's Journal*) to ask its editor, Lev Jan Palda, for advice. His assistant told them the boss wasn't in, but if they'd quietly head to the corner of Broadway and Forest Streets, Palda would meet them there.

A *Cleveland Plain Dealer* reporter accompanied them. He asked them what they'd do if Standard Oil shut them out. One replied, "Well, let 'em do it.… When we get to starving they can send us to the workhouse. We'll get bread for our work there anyhow." Palda arrived and told them not to give in. More importantly, they needed to stay peaceful.

Standard Oil said the pay cut was merely a rollback of a recent 10 percent increase they'd given, so it ought not to cause undue hardship. The superintendent, Samuel Andrews, told the *Cleveland Plain Dealer* that the wage per barrel produced had been reduced from ten to nine cents, not eight as the men claimed. During the winter, they'd been paid eleven cents per barrel. At present they were working only half the usual hours due to a lack of demand. Andrews pointed out that the company's books were open for anyone to look at if they wanted to see for themselves. The coopers demanded twelve cents a barrel.

The strike quickly expanded to additional businesses. Strikers headed to mills at the village of Newburgh Heights, where they convinced many to join. They also went to other cooper shops in Cleveland, where they found enthusiastic support. The addition of Cleveland's sewer workers didn't help their cause. More militant, they formed gangs and forced any men they saw working to stop, requiring police presence to protect those who wanted to continue with their jobs.

On April 27, newspapers reported that Standard Oil planned to move all barrel-making operations to Hunter's Point in Queens, now a borough of New York City. Oil refined in Cleveland would ship there in tank cars. To facilitate this, Standard had 250 new cars under construction. This was a bluff. Andrews later admitted that Standard had no intention of moving the barrel-making shops unless the strike forced it, though he did claim that the company had 450 tank cars being built just in case.

On the morning of May 2, Standard announced it had enough men willing to work for nine cents a barrel to open another barrel-making shop. Fearing those still striking would interfere, Andrews drew up a list of men who would agree to become special police to protect the shops. That evening, between ninety and one hundred men were sworn in. Issued badges, they were ordered to report for duty at the shops at five o'clock the next morning. Regular police also patrolled the grounds. On May 10, Standard issued a statement to its striking coopers—whom the press called "hoopers-off"—that if they didn't show up to work at Shops Two and Three, they would need to collect their tools by that Saturday.

The strike reached a crisis point that same day. Every day, several hundred strikers gathered outside the Standard works to continue their protest at the lower and upper gates. Up to one hundred regular policemen reinforced by three hundred volunteers served as guards. About one thousand strikers and their female partners showed up that morning. The women used clubs to assault coopers who passed the picket line.

Considering this a riot, the police ordered everyone to disperse. A prearranged signal was telegraphed to the fire department to request steam-powered fire engines so they could douse the crowd if the need arose. The police tried to push the crowd back, but it refused to move. The women started pounding on the fence and then sent a shower of stones and other readily available missiles at the police. The police produced their clubs and headed into the crowd. They prevailed, leaving a couple women severely beaten.

This incident took the fight out of the strike, which officially ended on May 14. The workers agreed to nine cents a barrel with the promise that wages would be raised for them and all Standard workers when the company's officers deemed it could afford to do so. The company also agreed to stop hiring boys.

The strike had spooked Cleveland's elite, and the Lake Shore strikers well knew that if violence broke out, it wouldn't go well for them. On the same day that Lake Shore workers issued their demands, men from their machine shops walked off the job with a demand of a 20 percent increase of their wages. With freight train traffic at a halt, Cleveland industries such as Cleveland Rolling Mill and Standard Oil shuttered most of their operations because they couldn't move their products out of the city. Freight cars piled up for miles. Perishable goods went bad. One source says that Lake Shore men offloaded three hundred carloads of pigs and cattle to herd them into pens where they were cared for. Another claimed that one hundred hogs died of thirst, and the cattle were taken to Painesville. Strikers allowed passenger trains to run.

The Lake Shore strike inspired those working at the nearby Cleveland, Columbus, Cincinnati & Indianapolis Railroad to also walk off the job over a planned pay cut. This road was incorporated on March 12, 1845, as the Cleveland, Columbus & Cincinnati. It began operations on February 22, 1851, with a total of 138 miles of track. A merger with the Indianapolis & Bellefontaine Railroad extended its reach to Indianapolis, giving it a total of 391 miles of track. It also changed its name to the Cleveland, Columbus, Cincinnati & Indianapolis. In 1871, it leased the Cincinnati & Springfield Railway to give it a connection to Springfield, Ohio.

Upon hearing that some of his workers had struck, the road's president, John H. Devereux, left his office to address them. He said that rate wars among all the roads had resulted in the wage cuts and promised to increase

John H. Devereux, circa 1861–65. *Library of Congress Prints and Photographs.*

wages by 10 percent on August 1. He asked them to swear that they'd participate in no more labor actions and would, if called upon by the authorities, help stop disturbances including riots. Every man there took the oath.

That Devereux compromised with his workers might come as a surprise considering doing so was seen by many at the time as the first step toward communism. Certainly nothing in Devereux's background suggests that he'd be no less ruthless toward his employees than any of the other railroad presidents. Born in Boston, Massachusetts, in 1832, Devereux traced his ancestry all the way back to William the Conqueror. At the age of sixteen, he moved to Cleveland, where he worked as a civil engineer on the same road he later headed. In 1852, he left for Tennessee to serve as an engineer on the Tennessee & Alabama Railroad. During the Civil War, he oversaw the repairing of tracks, buildings, and equipment in warzones.

In 1864, Devereux became general superintendent of the Cleveland & Pittsburgh Railroad. In 1868, he became a vice president of the Lake Shore and then its president. When it consolidated with the Michigan Southern, he was made the consolidated road's general manager. He became president of the Cleveland, Columbus, Cincinnati & Indianapolis in 1873 while at the same time being put in charge of the troubled Atlantic & Great Western Railway, whose employees didn't strike because their wages hadn't been reduced.

Devereux had a philosophy that the main purpose of a railroad was to serve the public first and make a profit second. Although strict with his employees, he was also reasonable and tried to do nothing unjust toward them. He considered himself their friend. He didn't stand for dereliction of duty, but anyone, no matter their position, could visit him in his office. If they had a legitimate grievance, he'd sort it out.

Lake Shore strikers promised not to interfere with Devereux's men returning to work. That didn't stop them from sending a committee of one hundred made up primarily of brakemen and firemen west to Toledo to agitate the Lake Shore employees there. Arriving on July 25 at about

"Lake Shore Limited in Train Yard, Union Depot, Toledo." Postcard, circa 1911. *Author's collection.*

one o'clock in the afternoon, they detrained and then ordered their fellow employees to stop working. They willingly complied. Urging their Toledo compatriots to remain peaceful, the Cleveland men led them to the Middle Grounds.

This was the place at which incoming lake, train, and vehicular traffic came to unload or take goods from warehouses. Boardinghouses and hotels accommodated all the transient workers here, and a church held services for sailors and railroaders. The strikers stopped all but a single pony engine from running, which was used to assemble passenger trains.

Toledo Mayor William W. Jones supported the strikers. A physician and surgeon by trade, he was born on September 28, 1819, in New York. He began his working life a journalist, moved to Ohio in 1836 to run a flour mill with his brother in Dresden, and then began studying medicine. Graduating from the University of Buffalo in 1844, he moved to Toledo to set up a practice. Fortuitously for its residents, he proved to be an exceptional physician when a cholera epidemic broke out in the city that summer. He was also a talented surgeon and performed the first lithotomy (the removal of stones from the urinary tract, bladder, or kidneys) in northwest Ohio. At the time of the strike, he was serving his third nonconsecutive term as Toledo's mayor.

An Ohio National Guardsman stationed in the city, Colonel Henry G. Neubert, didn't like the look of the crowds forming throughout the city and felt the mayor failed to recognize their potential to get out of hand. He was dismayed that Jones was not inclined to use the police to ensure things stayed peaceful and was astounded that the mayor didn't mind that the guardsmen in the city were relocating to their camp along Maumee Bay. The mayor, Neubert wrote in an official report, believed the Guard's presence "*might excite* [his emphasis] the strikers."

The next day, demonstrators threatened the Board of Trade, erroneously believing it was behind the recent increase in the price of flour. Jones reacted by calling a meeting at Market Space that afternoon. He lost control of the crowd, and it turned into a mob that gutted the Board of Trade's building. Toledo was shut down. Jones declared that anyone out after ten o'clock at night would be arrested. Saloons were closed.

Sheriff Albert Moore organized the city's citizens into a civilian peacekeeping force. Volunteers assembled into companies at Boody House. Overall command was given to Neubert. He sent out sixty young men to patrol the streets that night, splitting them into three groups and taking personal command of one. He received intelligence from a city detective that the Fenians—an Irish organization outlawed in its homeland that held the goal of gaining Ireland's independence from the United Kingdom—had hidden a cache of arms and ammunition that they'd once used for a raid into Canada. Neubert's men searched and found it. It consisted of 365 guns and two thousand rounds of ammunition.

The next day, saloons remained closed. James Turney, the man who'd organized the demonstration at the Board of Trade, was arrested and thrown into the county jail. Other arrests rapidly followed. Jones issued a proclamation that the incitement of riots wouldn't be tolerated. All men who wished to work would be allowed to.

On July 27, the Ohio National Guard under Neubert was asked to return from its camp and aid in patrolling the streets to keep the peace. The Guard in coordination with the citizen's militia gathered at the courthouse at 8:30 a.m. on August 2. With the police in the lead and two pieces of artillery at the rear, they headed to the Middle Grounds. The guns were placed to command the area in case the strikers there made trouble. This show of strength ended the strike. A pony engine was pulled out of a roundhouse, signaling the resumption of train traffic.

Similar disturbances occurred all across Ohio. On July 23, a crowd of about two thousand men assembled in front of a new hotel being built in

Zanesville. They ordered its construction workers to cease their labor, with violence being the alternative. The crowd, better characterized as a mob, moved to the courthouse, where Henry Blandy spoke to the group and suggested that they allow the upcoming Democratic convention to address their concerns. Uninterested, the mob forced various manufacturers to shut down or face the destruction of their property. Streetcars operated by Townsend & Burgess were also made to cease operation.

The mayor, William H. McOwen, ordered all the city's saloons closed. A vigilante committee consisting of about one thousand citizens formed. Well-armed, it arrested twenty-five men who were considered the leaders of the mob, one of whom was said to have come from Pittsburgh. Most of the city's workers didn't endorse the violence and had acquiesced to the strike for fear that their employers' properties would be damaged. The streetcars resumed running by the afternoon of July 24.

Columbus had a similar experience. On July 22, a mob made up mostly of opportunists and not strikers stopped a Panhandle Railroad train. That afternoon, firemen and brakemen of the Panhandle met at Goodale Park, where they decided to meet formally at the Union Depot that evening. Several thousand from the Panhandle and the Baltimore & Ohio attended, and they decided to strike. The most radical speech of the night came from Milton Spohn, who warned there could be violence to secure workers' rights.

The *Newark Advocate* reported that a mob between two and three hundred, consisting mainly "of tramps, miners and idle roughs," forced many of the city's mills and factories to close the next day. Those who resisted were threatened with arson. They recruited men from these places, and at noon about two thousand of them stopped at Union Depot to eat lunch from their pails. Afterward, they forced more factories to close. They offered nothing more than threats, so no violence erupted. All the railroads in the city stopped operations to avoid being shut down by the mob.

That evening, incensed citizens of Columbus met, and about five hundred of them joined a special police force. Their presence in the city the next day allowed most of the shuttered businesses to reopen, although the strike itself continued. On the morning of July 28, Mayor John H. Heitmann led twenty policemen toward the Little Miami Railroad to get its trains running. Along the way, his force picked up soldiers returning from Newark who had been ordered to offer their support.

As a crowd watched, a freight train was assembled. Strikers tried to entice its crew to abandon the effort, including offering its engineer $100 to desist, but with no effect. The train departed at about eleven o'clock that

Above: Union Station in Columbus. Detroit Publishing Co., circa 1904. *Library of Congress Prints and Photographs.*

Left: Columbus Mayor John Henry Heitmann. From the *Columbus Citizen-Journal*, circa 1878. *Columbus Metropolitan Library (Ohio).*

morning. A second freight train was accompanied by soldiers for the first few miles. Strikers stopped it at Alton Station, but soldiers headed there and got it moving.

On July 29, Colonel Samuel Smith led several Ohio National Guard companies to the yard of the Columbus, Piqua & Indianapolis Railroad to reinforce guardsmen already there. Smith wrote in his report that they had to deal with "a disorderly crowd, consisting of from fifteen hundred to two thousand persons." Strikers put out the fire of an engine as it headed to couple itself to a train, so Smith put it under his men's protection. Had the fire stayed out and the engine cooled off, it would have taken up to thirty-six hours to get the water temperature in its tank back to boiling.

With guardsmen on either side, the engine moved toward the train to which it was to be coupled. As it neared a switch, it was derailed by a coal car pushed in its way by a group of five strikers. Smith ordered his men to arrest those responsible, but all save for one escaped in the gathering crowd of onlookers. The crowd attempted to rescue the prisoner, but Smith called more men over, and they kept them from doing so.

A strike in the village of Crestline was quite different than those in Toledo, Zanesville, and Columbus. It began when two engines were forced into the workshops. The next morning, firemen and brakemen told the shops to close. The track men and those in the freight house joined as well. The men stayed peaceful and made it a point not to harm company property. Meetings were held in Diamond Hall. The strike ended on July 31. Crestline Mayor Edwin Booth issued a proclamation on August 2 thanking the people of the village and especially the strikers for their "good conduct."

CHAPTER 8

AUTHORITY STRIKES BACK

Cincinnati served as the eastern terminus for the Ohio & Mississippi Railroad, which connected Ohio to St. Louis and was the road by which Baltimore & Ohio Railroad freight and passengers continued west. On July 23, its men struck, blocking both freight and passenger trains. Only postal cars were allowed to leave the yards. A mob of people not associated with the railroad invaded the yards. One of its members, Charles Ashby, ordered fireman Mr. Fagaley and engineer John McMillan to take Engine No. 106 to the roundhouse while Ashby and a confederate named Red Morris tried to destroy railroad equipment and tracks.

Ashby, John "Buck" Mullaney, and William Patterson were arrested as the heads of this mob. They were incarcerated at the Ninth Street Police Station, and a crowd marched up there and demanded the release of Mullaney. Charles Jacob, vice president of the Board of Aldermen, warned them to disperse in ten minutes or less. They refused, so police swept up Central and Ninth Streets and chased them away.

At about eleven o'clock that night, a mob attempted to burn the Ohio & Mississippi Railroad bridge over Mill Creek at Front and Sixth Streets. The mob had broken into McDonald's Oil Factory and rolled barrels of coal oil to the bridge. They poured it over the rafters and added tar, then set it afire. Police and firemen arrived, but the mob interfered with the latter by cutting their hoses and assaulting at least two of them. The fire was put out. The mob threatened ten policemen, but reinforcements prevented violence.

Early the next morning, the bridge was set on fire again, this conflagration engulfing a freight car. It, too, was put out, and police began guarding both ends of the bridge, which had suffered severe damage. The mob also looted milk and market wagons heading into the city for the day. One of the rioters, eighteen-year-old Benjamin Butler, was arrested and charged with inciting the mob, as were William Whalan, Oliver Parker, and George Dearing.

Tramps and thieves were blamed for the destruction, not strikers. On the same day as this incident, the Board of Police Commissioners called on citizens to form companies of fifty men. These volunteers had to bring their own weapons because the Police Board had none to hand out, although Police Superintendent Ira Wood set about remedying this.

That afternoon, another mob formed consisting of boys and men from between thirteen and twenty-one years of age. They surrounded the depot of the Cincinnati, Hamilton & Dayton Railroad. As a train readied to depart, a young man climbed onto it, uncoupled the engine, and pulled the throttle. Fortunately, its engineer was nearby, and he jumped on board and stopped it before something awful occurred. Members of the mob, who said they weren't railroaders, demanded that the shop close and then went into the yard and forced employees there to cease working. The railroad men acceded but stressed that they'd only stopped because they were being forced to. The mob also stopped the Marietta & Cincinnati Railroad's trains from running.

Cincinnati, Hamilton & Dayton Locomotive 210. Postcard, circa 1907–15. *Author's collection.*

An editorial from the *Catholic Organ* reprinted in the July 27 edition of the *Cincinnati Commercial* blamed the destruction of property in Cincinnati on communists, claiming that the most outspoken of this breed were saloonkeepers. While it's doubtful such a sweeping indictment had any validity, this does bring up a good question. What was the motivation of the mobs that set the Ohio & Mississippi bridge on fire and stopped trains on the Marietta & Cincinnati from running?

Media sources of the day claimed they were mainly tramps—meaning the unemployed. Cincinnati's mayor, Robert M. Moore, asked the mob at the Cincinnati, Hamilton & Dayton's depot this: What was the point of burning buildings? Someone answered, "It would show that we are men." In other words, they were taking out their frustrations against the forces beyond their control that had created the economic depression.

On July 27, a citizens' police force dispersed a mob trying to stop trains on the Cincinnati, Hamilton & Dayton Railroad. On the same day, another crowd tried to halt a Dayton & Cincinnati Short Line train by intimidating its engineer. A frustrated ex-railroader pulled out his pistol and threatened to shoot the first man who interfered with the train's operation. No one did. Strikers became annoyed by these opportunists causing unnecessary trouble and destroying property. Sometimes unsavory individuals preyed on the strikers themselves. At one of their rallies, a pickpocket relieved many of them of their valuables, including a gold watch owned by an engineer.

All these disturbances prompted Ohio Governor Thomas L. Young to issue an order on July 25 calling on citizens to form volunteer police forces to deal with them. Born on December 14, 1832, in Killyleagh County, Ireland, Young moved to the United States at an early age. Raised in New York City, he joined the U.S. Army at the age of sixteen. While a sergeant in the Third Artillery, he sailed to California on the steamer *San Francisco* with his wife and child in late December 1854. A terrible storm overtook the vessel, during which the *San Francisco* lost its engine and foremast. A single wave swept about 150 passengers overboard, and by the time of the *San Francisco*'s rescue, over 300 were dead. Young's wife and child survived the voyage but later died from the effects of exposure. Young rarely spoke about the incident.

During the Civil War, he trained a company of Cincinnati Home Guard who never saw service. In August 1861, he was made a captain in General John C. Frémont's bodyguard until it was disbanded by General Henry Halleck on January 1, 1862. Now a civilian, Young served as the editor of a Democratic newspaper in Sydney, Ohio, and then rejoined the Union army

PULLMAN
Compartment Cars
CINCINNATI,
INDIANAPOLIS,
CHICAGO.
CINCINNATI HAMILTON & DAYTON R.R.
CH&D
CINCINNATI
INDIANAPOLIS CHICAGO DAYTON TOLEDO DETROIT
THROUGH TRAINS
CINCINNATI,
DAYTON,
TOLEDO,
DETROIT.
"WING SHOT"
ORIENTAL POWDER MILLS
MOSLER SAFE Co.
WHISKY
THE CINCINNATI TIMES-STAR
LARGEST MAKERS OF FOUR TO FIFTEEN PASSENGER VEHICLES IN THE WORLD. OVER ONE HUNDRED ELEGANT STYLES OF TWO AND FOUR WHEELERS. PRICES THE LOWEST.
The COOK CARRIAGE Co.
CINCINNATI, OHIO.
INTERIOR OF DINING CARS ON THE
CINCINNATI, HAMILTON & DAYTON R.R.

in August of that same year. Given the rank of major, he was put in charge of recruiting a company for the 118th Ohio Infantry. He became its provost marshal when it took to the field. Promoted to lieutenant colonel in February 1864, he was made a full colonel that same year.

Poor health forced him to resign in September 1864. Despite this, President Abraham Lincoln made him a brevet brigadier general on March 13, 1865. Young moved to Cincinnati, where he studied law at Cincinnati Law College, from which he graduated in 1865 and made the city his home. Going into politics, he served in local and state-level offices, including the Ohio House of Representatives and Senate. He was Ohio's lieutenant governor from 1875 to 1877 under Rutherford Hayes, whose resignation in 1877 to take the office of U.S. president elevated Young to the role of governor.

Rather than head to Cincinnati to help deal with the disturbances there, Young focused his attention on the crisis at Newark, a city east of Columbus through which the Baltimore & Ohio and Panhandle Railroads' trains both passed. The Panhandle was a subsidiary of the Pennsylvania Railroad, which made Newark one of the most important railroad centers in the state where trains belonging to the nation's biggest carriers traveled in all four cardinal directions. The Baltimore & Ohio also owned about ten acres of land there on which stood repair shops, roundhouses, and track sidings. If you wanted to maximize the stoppage of train traffic on both roads, there was no better place in Ohio.

Opposite: This ad published in 1894 shows the interior of a Pullman car for the Cincinnati, Hamilton & Dayton Railroad. Strobridge & Co. Lith Co. *Library of Congress Prints and Photographs.*

Above: Thomas L. Young, circa 1865–80. *Library of Congress Prints and Photographs.*

The strike in Newark began on July 18 when Baltimore & Ohio brakemen and firemen stopped a freight train at ten o'clock that night. About 10 percent of Newark's population worked for the railroads, and they had the broad support of the town's citizens. The strikers allowed passenger and mail trains to pass through.

By noon the next day, the yard contained 225 cars and 75 idle engines, a number increased by the arrival of two more Baltimore & Ohio trains. Management

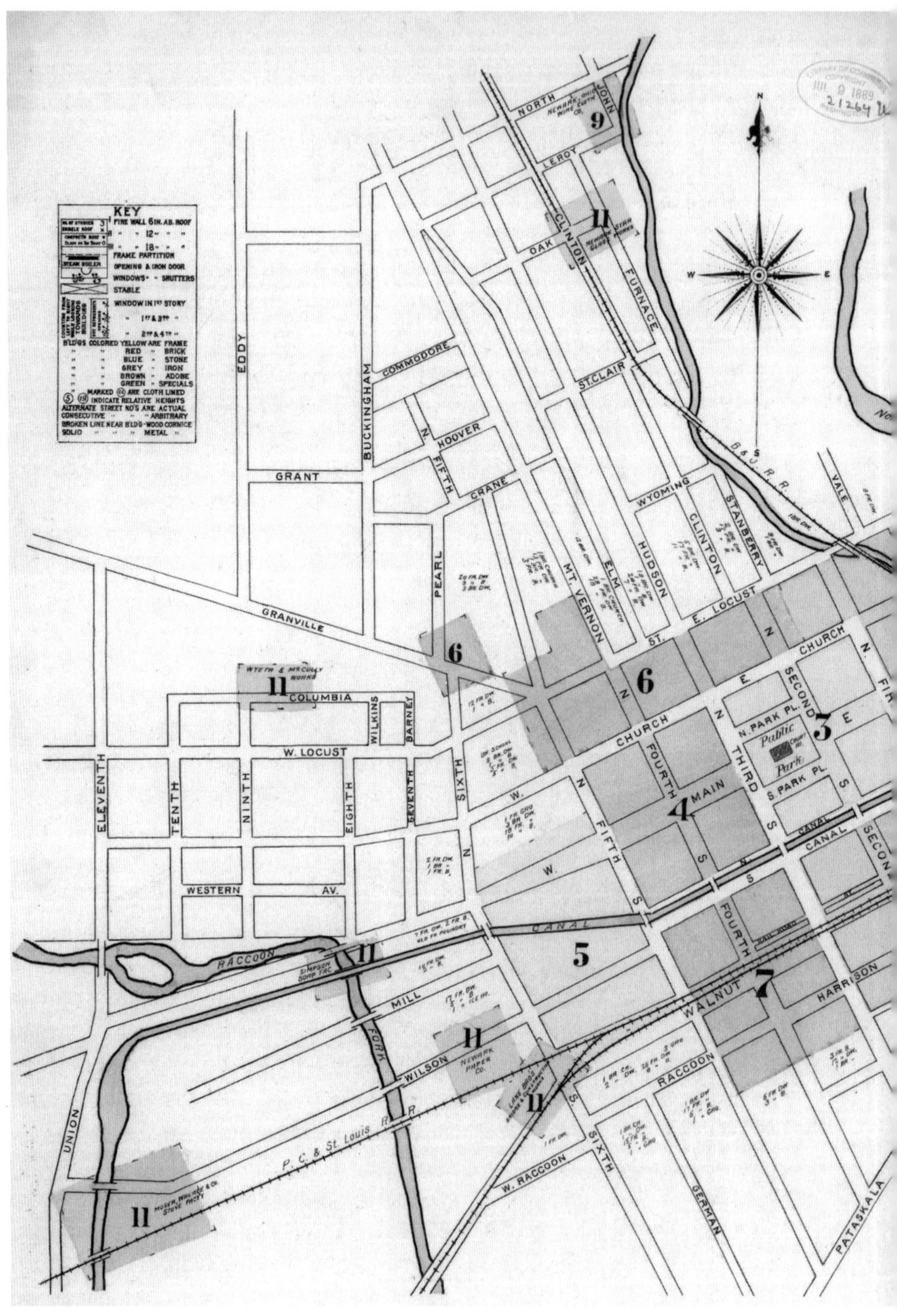
KEY
NORTH
JOHN
LEROY
OAK
CLINTON
FURNACE
EDDY
BUCKINGHAM
COMMODORE
ST.CLAIR
HOOVER
FIFTH
GRANT
CRANE
WYOMING
CLINTON
STANBERRY
VALE
B. & O. R.R.
PEARL
MT. VERNON
ELM
HUDSON
E. LOCUST
GRANVILLE
CHURCH
SECOND
WYETH & McCULLY WORKS
COLUMBIA
WILKINS
BARNEY
W. LOCUST
N. PARK PL.
Public Park
S. PARK PL.
ELEVENTH
TENTH
NINTH
EIGHTH
SEVENTH
SIXTH
FOURTH
MAIN
THIRD
FIFTH
CANAL
WESTERN AV.
RACCOON
MILL
WALNUT
HARRISON
WILSON
NEWARK PAPER CO.
RACCOON
UNION
P. C. & St. Louis R.R.
MOSER, WALKER & CO. STOVE FACT'Y
W. RACCOON
SIXTH
GERMAN
PATASKALA
N
S
E
W
9
11
6
3
4
5
7

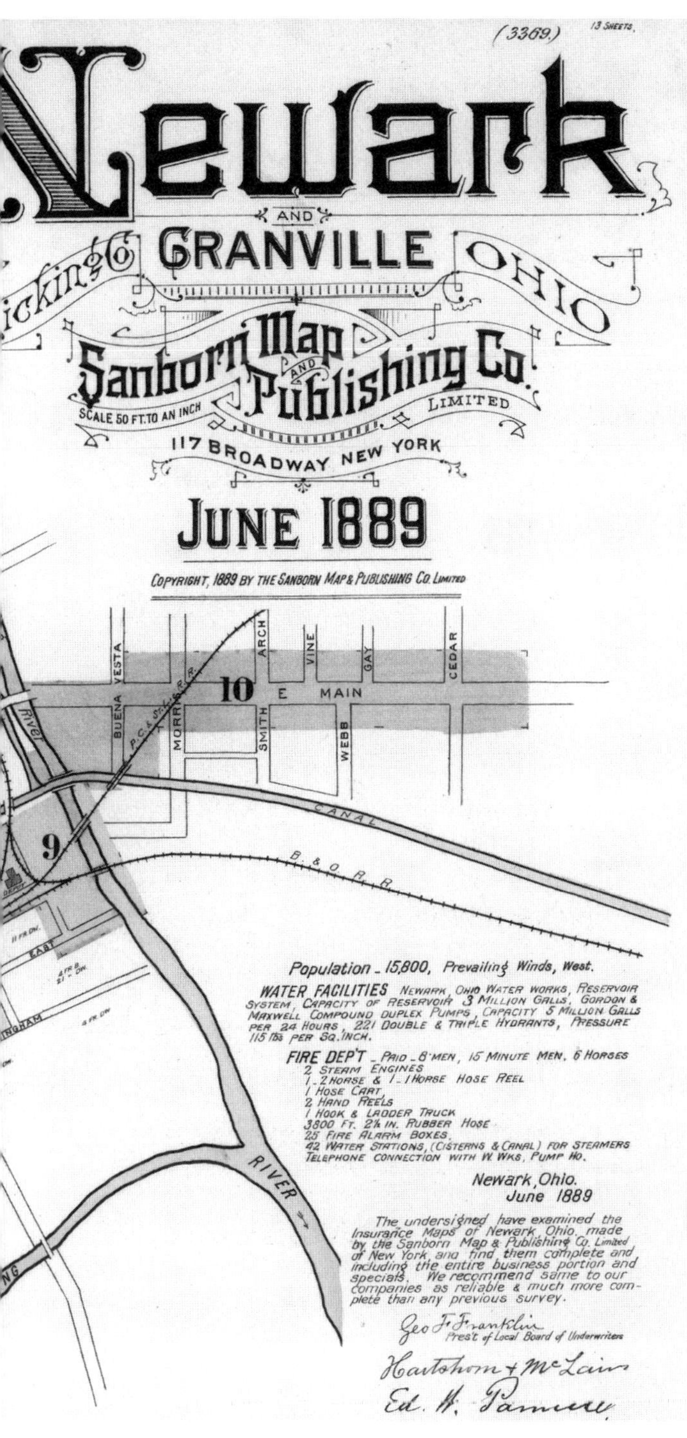

An 1889 Sanborn fire insurance map of Newark. *Library of Congress Geography and Map Division.*

nonetheless tried to get something moving. The *Newark Advocate* reported that Frank Brown, who had once served on the Newark City Council and had worked for the Baltimore & Ohio, volunteered to be a fireman. As he climbed aboard, strikers approached. A striking fireman held up his hand to show he lacked three fingers. A spokesman for the strikers informed Brown, "This is the man whose place you are taking. This man who works with a hand and a half to earn $1.50 a day, three days a week, for his wife and children. Do you propose to take the bread out of his mouth and theirs?" Brown climbed down, eliciting three cheers from the crowd.

On July 20, Licking County Sheriff Samuel H. Schofield and the yard's master of transportation, Mr. Frank, came to the Baltimore & Ohio yards. Frank told a reporter he'd put the sheriff in charge and aimed to start up a train. About an hour later, a train driven by engineer David Loughery started down the track. About two hundred to three hundred men consisting of strikers and citizens surrounded the engine. Sheriff Schofield began speaking to the crowd, but it made so much noise that no one heard anything but his conclusion, in which he told them they were violating Ohio laws and he'd see to it that property was protected.

To this, one striker, Albert Lynn, replied, "We don't blame you, Mr. Schofield…but we can't stand this. I've got a wife and two children now suffering for victuals. I'll stand this thing as long as I've got a drop of blood in my heart." Upon learning this, Loughery kicked the engine loose from the cars and abandoned it. Schofield sent a message to Governor Young asking for him to send the Ohio National Guard to keep order. The next day, Baltimore & Ohio officials attempted to contact both Young and Ohio's adjutant general, Charles W. Carr, but neither was in Columbus. When someone finally reached the governor, he promised to be back in Columbus the next day but made no commitments as to what he would do. He refused to call in federal troops, insisting he'd never do that unless every last Ohio Guardsman was "whipped."

The men of the Panhandle joined with their Baltimore & Ohio brethren. On July 22, strikers from Dennison arrived in the city. Miners from the area offered to give their assistance if called up. The strikers sent a committee to Columbus to ask workers there to join the strike. That night, the strikers in Newark itself met to draw up their demands, which included rescinding the recent wage cut.

A train carrying 170 Ohio National Guardsmen arrived from Columbus at 12:30 a.m. on July 21. Young had chosen troops from Circleville, Mount Vernon, Springfield, and Zanesville because they were the only guardsmen with breechloading rifles. He and Carr arrived on the same train. He planned to negotiate with the strikers. The next night, more troops arrived.

On the morning of July 22, Young and his staff met with the Guard's company commanders and railroad officials to decide the next course of action. The officials informed Young that they had brakemen and firemen willing to work at the lower wages on offer if the railroad yard were cleared, so a plan was formed to accomplish this objective. Guardsmen from Zanesville would protect westbound trains while those from Mount Vernon would clear the yard itself. It became apparent that the train cars were too close together for the plan to work without more men. Young feared if the guardsmen tried to execute it with their current strength, it might result in violence, so he called in reinforcements from Cincinnati and Dayton.

Arriving in the early hours of the next morning, the reinforcements' officers spent the night at a hotel, leaving their enlisted men on the trains, a trying experience for the latter because they erroneously believed the strikers planned to attack them. With about 530 troops at his disposal, Young ordered the strikers to clear the yard by six o'clock that morning. The strikers didn't move, so the Fourth Regiment's Colonel Samuel Smith (who we met in Columbus in the previous chapter) decided to cross the bridge to the yards. He left a detachment behind under the command of Lieutenant Maurice Holden to keep anyone from following. Holden and his men had to contend with about 200 strikers demanding to be allowed to cross the bridge as was their right because it was for public use.

Additional strikers outflanked the guardsmen and headed into the yards. Assistant Adjutant General Daniel Grosvenor arrived and told the strikers to disband. They refused, so he went to the surgeon's quarters to secure the bandages needed for what he expected to be a bloody affair. Fortunately, Captain Alden Steel, commander of the Champion City Guard, realized that although the strikers had refused his order as well, it wasn't quite as dire a situation as Grosvenor saw it. Colonel Smith agreed, and by eleven o'clock that morning, the strikers had dispersed on their own. The guards took control of the yard, but the strike continued.

The next day, July 23, reports reached Newark that men from the New Straitsville and Shawnee mines had seized trains and were headed for the city to support the strikers. It turned out no *miners* were on board a single train, but rather it carried a citizens' committee from Shawnee coming to investigate what was happening in Newark. A quick consultation with a Newark-based citizens' committee set them straight, so they headed home.

W.C. Quincey, Baltimore & Ohio's Trans-Division manager, informed Governor Young that he felt the guardsmen could go home. Young sent all but those under the command of Captain Steel home on July 28. By July 30, he felt he could end the strike peacefully and brought in over one thousand guardsmen to ensure the trains started moving after the Baltimore & Ohio brought in strikebreakers to resume operations. With guardsmen on board, fourteen trains rolled out of the city on August 1.

That same day, Colonel Charles B. Hunt returned to Newark with five companies. Arriving at around two o'clock that afternoon, he received word that two freight trains were expected from Dennison at about 7:25 p.m. He sent men to guard all the town's switches and waited. When the trains failed to show up, he and some of his men boarded a passenger train heading east to investigate. Roughly a mile and a half into the trip, they found the trains on sidings put there by strikers who, upon seeing the soldiers, dispersed. Hunt waited until the next morning to get them moving. There were no further issues.

The people of Ohio at first supported the strikes, but as they dragged on, sentiment changed not because they didn't think the workers had good reasons for them but because Ohioans were being seriously inconvenienced. Passenger trains, as an example, might still be running, but they faced chronic delays. According to an Ohio government report, "Supplies of every kind were growing scarce in the cities; factories and manufacturing establishments were beginning to close for want of raw materials, and facilities for shipping their wares, and filling their orders and contracts." Seasonal produce couldn't be moved. Even some of the strikers wearied of it and were willing to return to work whether or not their demands were met.

New York City gives us an example of the impact that the strikes had on everyday life. Usually an average of five hundred cars of cattle carrying nine thousand head arrived there every week during the summer. With the trains stopped in Pittsburgh and also in Buffalo, some of the city's butchers ran out of meat to sell. Scarcity drove up prices. In just a couple days, the price of beef rose from 11.5 cents per pound to 14. Mutton increased from 10 to 15 cents, and lamb went from 12.5 to 17 cents. The only good news was that during the hot weather, meat was in far less demand in the city than during the cooler months, so people might not mind going without.

Despite the chaos and fear the strikes created, one enterprising Ohio business, Moses Black's Dry Goods Store on Main and Market Streets in Mansfield, placed an ad in the *Mansfield Herald* with the lead: "The Great Strike! Not for Higher Wages but a Strike for Lower Prices." The sale would last from July 25 to September 1 and claimed that the store would sell "Dry Goods at Cost!"

The strikes started winding down on July 25. Some Baltimore & Ohio freight trains began running on July 27, and on July 29, a doubleheader Pennsylvania Railroad train left Pittsburgh. Most strikes ended by July 30. It's estimated that 500,000 workers from a variety of industries had walked off the job. The resulting violence left 11 dead in Baltimore, 42 in Pittsburgh, 12 in Reading, and many more elsewhere for a total of over 100. Thanks in part to Governor Young's leadership, no deaths and little violence or property damage occurred in Ohio.

CHAPTER 9

THE AFTERMATH

The strikes spooked those in power, prompting them to increase the size of police forces and strengthen state militias. Some cities created new militias. Although violence hadn't erupted in Cleveland, the city's elite nonetheless engineered the formation of the First Troop of Light Cavalry, known as Troop A, and the Cleveland Gatling Gun Battery. Troop A was set up on October 10, 1877, with forty-one members. Its first armory, built on Euclid Avenue for $3,100 (just over $91,000 today), was replaced twice, once in 1885 and again in 1923. The Cleveland Gatling Gun Battery formed in June 1878. It had twenty-five men and two Gatling guns, which fortunately were never used against the citizens of Cleveland or anyone else.

Not everyone thought more militias were the answer to future unrest. In a piece written for the August 1877 edition of the magazine *Evolution*, J.D. Bell opined, "Our militia is useless, its organization faulty, its members without experience or discipline, and its officers without control over their men or knowledge of military affairs. The firing into peaceable crowds and running away from a belligerent mob are alike disgraceful to any body calling itself military." What was needed, he argued, was a vastly enlarged U.S. Army capable of keeping order and protecting life and property. Bell understood the reasons for the strikes and compared the overall lack of sympathy for them to the way abolitionists had been treated during the runup to the Civil War.

The majority of American media sided with capital and demonized labor and its plight. One major exception to that was the *Crestline Advocate*. Admittedly, it did serve a railroad town and the strikers were peaceful, but it clearly favored the railroaders:

> *Many of our prominent citizens have been present at the meetings of the railroad men, and all who have been called upon to express their views regarding the strike, sympathize with them. The strikers here are known to be among our best citizens, and many of them have large families to support, but find it a difficult matter so to do at the present state of wages, and we hope the matter will be speedily adjusted. The business of our place is materially affected, and almost at a standstill.*

The magazine *Christian Union* well understood the reasons for the strikes, but it had no sympathy for the men who'd walked off their jobs. The magazine saw their demands as communistic in nature and asserted that higher wages resulted in higher prices. To deal with reduced hours, it suggested in an August 11 editorial that "so long as there is only half work to be done, either they must all be content to work on half time or half of them must resign all wages to give full wages to those that remain." Those who obstructed the railroads ought to be punished, and those railroads that had given into workers' demands had committed a grave error.

The September 1877 article "The Communist and the Railway" in *International Review* had a similar view. It deemed the claim by railroad workers that they couldn't live on their current wages a lie, certain they could find another job that paid more. Indeed, "there is today no other place on earth in which labor, requiring so little of training or intelligence, can earn as high wages as in the positions of fireman and brakeman on American railways." Laborers didn't have the right to "rob the rich" just so they could buy things not absolutely necessary to live. The rights of property should supersede the needs of the railroad laborer who wanted pay raises or farmers who wanted lower freight rates.

The unnamed writer of this article argued that the destruction of Pittsburgh was caused by communism getting a foothold in the United States. Rhetoric like this sparked what is possibly America's first red scare. The depression of the 1870s prompted a large swath of Americans to consider accepting what socialism had to offer for the first time in the nation's history. This in turn created a panic that communism would sweep across the streets of America, resurrecting memories of France's short-lived Paris Commune. This unplanned experiment had occurred six years earlier and was sparked by circumstances quite different than what led to the Great Railroad Strike of 1877.

The road to the Commune began in 1848 when the French people forced King Louis Philippe into exile and then replaced their constitutional monarchy with what has since been called the Second French Republic. Napoléon Bonaparte's nephew Louis Napoléon Bonaparte was elected its president, but in 1852, he declared himself emperor, ushering in the Second Empire.

At that time, thousands of French peasants had moved into Paris to work in its factories, and the neighborhoods in which they lived were dismal. Louis Napoléon decided to implement urban renewal, which resulted in the destruction of about twenty thousand buildings containing 100,000 apartments. Now the poor had to cram themselves into the northern and eastern neighborhoods. About a fourth of all Parisians lived in poverty, this at a time when the city had just over one million people. The poor watched the city's wealthy and the royal court live extravagantly on a daily basis.

Napoleon III, completely oblivious to the needs of his people, worried more about Prussia and declared war on that kingdom on July 19, 1870. His reign and the Second Empire ended on September 2, 1870, when he and the army he led (rather badly, it must be said) surrendered to the Prussians. On September 4, the Government of National Defense was formed, marking the beginning of the Third Republic. But its founding didn't end the war. The Prussians laid siege to Paris. It was up to the National Guard, which was more a police force than a proper army, to hold them off. With food supplies cut off, animals of all sorts, including rodents and those in the zoo, were eaten.

Louis Napoléon Bonaparte. Currier & Ives, circa 1849. *Library of Congress Prints and Photographs.*

The siege lasted four months and was lifted only when the government surrendered, giving some of France's territory away in the bargain and paying the Prussians 5 billion francs.

Parisians, who'd held the Prussians off all this time, weren't happy about it. A new conservative government under Adolphe Thiers made the situation worse. The tensions between his government and the National Guard came to a head when the regular army tried to purloin the Guard's artillery. The Guard not only prevented this, but it also chased Thiers and his government out of the city to the Palace of Versailles. The Paris Commune, supported by the Guard, was declared on March 28, 1871.

The Commune planned to establish a secular education system free for all with female teachers making the same as their male counterparts. Bakeries were banned from working at night, and bread prices fixed. Caps were put on rents and prices. State pawnshops were regulated. Pensions were given to the common-law wives of National Guardsmen killed during the fighting. Only church property was confiscated, and until the last week of its existence, the Commune destroyed no buildings or monuments.

One of its key leaders, Jules Bergeret, told American journalist Alvan S. Southworth that if the Commune fell, he'd make sure to blow up the Louvre and Tuileries Palace. When that day came, Bergeret changed his mind, ordering that the fires started in those locations be put out. This saved his life. When Thiers learned that Bergeret had protected the Louvre, instead of having him executed, he allowed him to escape to Belgium in disguise. Southworth fell afoul of the Commune and nearly lost his life to a firing squad. He was saved at the last minute by the American minister, Elihu Benjamin Washburne.

The Versailles government retook the city by force, an action that killed an estimated ten thousand Communards by the time the conflict ended on May 28. What terrified middle- and upper-class Americans most about the Commune was its destruction of property, such as the Vendôme Column, a monument to Napoléon Bonaparte's achievements that he built using captured bronze cannons. This particular act of vandalism prompted the *New York Herald* to editorialize, "If they [the Communards] burned the Hotel [*sic*] de Ville and leveled the Tuileries, they could not give the world better proof of what they are and what they mean. The fall of the Commune, which is now imminent, will be a relief to the whole civilized world."

Fear of communism didn't seem to enter the minds of Ohio's Republican Party when its delegates assembled in Cleveland on August 1 to form the party's platform for the upcoming fall elections. The convention adopted one that included opposition to further funding for railroads with public money, including a prohibition on giving them public land or renewing their land patents. The platform further called for Congress to establish a National

Parisian deputies such as those seen here were elected to represent their city district in the Commune for two years. 1871. *Library of Congress Prints and Photographs.*

Vendôme Column. Illustrated by Louis-Julien Jacottet, circa 1845–60. *Library of Congress Prints and Photographs.*

William H. West, the Republican candidate for the Ohio governor's race in 1877, ran on a platform that was accused of being communist by some Ohio newspapers. From *Bench and Bar of Ohio: A Compendium of History and Biography* (1897). *Wikimedia Commons.*

Bureau of Industry and to regulate railroads with powers that would "tend to promote safety of travel, secure fair returns for capital invested and fair wages for employees, preventing mismanagement, improper discrimination, and" stop railroad officials from enriching themselves "at the expense of the stockholders, shippers and employees." The convention nominated William H. West as its candidate for the upcoming governor's race.

West, born in Millsboro, Pennsylvania, on February 9, 1824, graduated from Jefferson College in 1846. He started out as a teacher in Kentucky, became a professor at Hampden-Sydney College in Prince Edward, Virginia, and then around 1850 moved to Bellefontaine, Ohio, where he studied law. He lived there until his death in 1914. He took a leadership role in the Republican Party at the age of thirty. During the Civil War, near-blindness and physical weakness prevented him from joining the military, so he served in the Ohio legislature and then as the state's attorney general from 1866 to 1868.

Shortly after his nomination, West addressed a Cleveland crowd that included former strikers. During his speech, he pointed out that he'd never owned railroad bonds and stocks and had no plans to. He proposed, "I would arrange and fix a minimum of prices for all who labor in the mines and upon the railroads, and then require that all the net receipts and proceeds of the capital invested, the laborer at the end of the year should, in addition to his fixed compensation receive a certain per cent. [*sic*] of the profits." He didn't know how he'd accomplish it, figuring it would be an experiment.

The *Cincinnati Enquirer* labeled the Republican platform "communistic." How dare it suggest that the federal government tell the railroads to run more safely, not to discriminate against certain businesses, and negotiate with its workers! Worse, if elected, West might establish a minimum wage in Ohio and make mines share their profits with the workers. Ohio voters weren't keen on these ideas either, and West lost to the Democratic candidate, Richard M. Bishop.

Richard M. Bishop, circa 1865–80. *Library of Congress Prints and Photographs.*

At the same time as Ohio's Republican Party planned for forthcoming election, trials for those arrested during the strikes went forward. Railroad officers figured that since many of the judges overseeing the courts were former railroad lawyers, they would happily make an example of those arrested. But most judges were wise enough to know that if they were too harsh, this might inflame tensions and reignite more unrest.

Of the hundreds arrested in Pittsburgh, most charges were dismissed, and those who did go to trial and were convicted received short sentences in workhouses. In Reading, only three out of sixty-three arrested were convicted. In Harrisburg, those convicted received only fines. For climbing onboard a locomotive in Cincinnati, John "Buck" Mullaney received a sentence of thirty days and was given a $500 fine plus another $500 as a bond to ensure he would not disturb the peace for the next year. Co-conspirator Charles Asby received the same sentence as Mullaney. Asby's jury trial and sentencing took just forty-five minutes. The cases of the men charged with burning the Ohio & Mississippi bridge—Oliver Park, William Whalen, and George Dearing—were dismissed.

Bankrupted railroads in receivership were under control of the government, so strikers prosecuted while working for them went to federal courts. A panel of three federal judges deemed those who struck were in contempt of court. This precedent set back organized labor for years.

While no major legislation at either the state or federal level resulted from the strikes to address the underlying issues that caused them, they were far more effective than some writers and historians give them credit for. The Marietta & Cincinnati agreed to rescind a wage cut when faced with the mere threat of a strike. So did the Cincinnati, Hamilton & Dayton Railroad. When its men promised to strike unless their 10 percent wage cut was reversed, the road's directors agreed not to implement it because its president, Robert M. Shoemaker, didn't want to see the destruction of company property. The Ohio & Mississippi also restored its old wage scale.

Although the Baltimore & Ohio never gave in, one of its vice presidents, William Keyser, introduced free boardinghouses for employees on overnight runs starting on August 30. President John Garrett, recognizing that his life had been in danger during the strike, also changed some policies. Railroad crews would no longer have to be on call for days at a time. Instead, they'd receive notice up to an hour before departure, and if the run were cancelled, they'd receive a quarter of the day's wages. In 1880, he established the Employees Relief Fund, into which workers paid a small amount each month in exchange for a guaranteed year's wages and indefinite time off to recover from injuries suffered while on duty. Other roads came up with similar benefits. Between 1877 and 1880, railroads also restored wage rates.

To deal with the problem of the ruinous rate cuts that had made wage reductions "necessary," railroad officials met at New York City's Metropolitan Hotel on September 27 to discuss the issue. Railroads presidents across the United States and Canada gathered at York City's Windsor Hotel to figure out the details. This meeting included the Baltimore & Ohio's Garrett, Erie Railroad's receiver Hugh J. Jewett, the Pennsylvania's Scott, New York Central's Vanderbilt, and the Grand Trunk's Sir Henry Tyler.

William Keyser was one of the Baltimore & Ohio Railroad's vice presidents. From *Men of Mark in Maryland*, vol. 1 (1907). *Wikimedia Commons.*

During the meeting, representatives of the Toledo, Wabash & Western complained that other roads had a secret monopoly on livestock transport to the eastern markets. Those participating in this deal charged $15 per carload, which amounted to about $3 million in traffic revenue, for which they paid $1 million to obtain. Despite the grumbling, Wall Street brokers were happy about the meeting because more profitable railroads meant higher stock prices. The trouble was, the deal had no mechanism of enforcement, and regulations wouldn't compel them to until Congress created the Interstate Commerce Commission in 1887. Rebates, a major part of the rate war problem, weren't outlawed until the passage of the Elkins Act in 1903.

ACKNOWLEDGEMENTS

There are quite a few people who gave me invaluable help who I'd like to thank, including: Kent Mulcahy, reference librarian, Geology and Local History Department, Cincinnati and Hamilton County Public Library; Mark Tidrick, subject department librarian, Cleveland Public Library; Ann Hurley, Local History and Genealogy Department, Toledo Lucas County Public Library; Scott Horst, Adult Services, Muskingum County Library System; Bill Fisher, Crestline Historical Society board member; and Gil Pietrzak, Carnegie Library of Pittsburgh, Pennsylvania Department.

I want to give a special thanks to Ed Stout, site manager of the Cooke-Dorn House in Sandusky, Ohio. He took time out of his busy schedule to give me a personal tour via an appointment. This is the house in which Jay Cooke's parents spent their remaining years.

BIBLIOGRAPHY

Databases

EBSCO: The Nation Digital Archive
Gale Primary Sources: Nineteenth-Century U.S. Newspapers
Gale Primary Sources: *The Economist*
Gale Virtual Reference Library
JSTOR
Library of Congress: Chronicling America
Mansfield/Richland County Public Library: Community History Archive
Newsbank: Cleveland Plain Dealer Historical and Current
Newspaper Archive
Newspapers.com
Ohio History Connection: Ohio Memory
Pennsylvania Newspaper Archive
Proquest Historical Newspapers: *Cincinnati Enquirer*
Proquest Historical Newspapers: *New York Times*
Western Pennsylvania History: 1918–2022

Books

Adams, Charles Francis, Jr. *Notes on Railroad Accidents.* G.P. Putman's Sons, 1879.

Aler, F. Vernon. *Aler's History of Martinsburg and Berkley County, West Virginia.* Mail Publishing Company, 1888.

American Social Science Association. *Proceedings of the Conference of Charities, Held in Connection with the General Meeting of the American Social Science Association, Saratoga, September, 1877.* Williams & Co., 1877.

Bellesiles, Michael A. *1877: America's Year of Living Violently*. New Press, 2010.

Brennan, Joseph Fletcher, ed. *The Biographical Cyclopedia and Portrait Gallery with an Historical Sketch of the State of Ohio.* Vol. 1. Western Biographical Publishing Company, 1883.

Cary, Ferdinand Ellsworth. *Lake Shore & Michigan Southern Railway System and Representative Employees: A History of the Development of the Lake Shore & Michigan Railway, from Its Inception, Together with Introductory and Supplementary Chapters…* Biographical Publishing Company, 1900.

Chernow, Ron. *Titan: The Life of John D. Rockefeller, Sr.* Random House, 1998.

Clarke, Thomas Curtis. *The American Railway: Its Construction, Development, Management, and Trains.* Skyhorse Publishing, 2012.

Cleveland, Columbus, Cincinnati and Indianapolis Railway Company. *Eighteenth Annual Report of the Board of Directors of the Cleveland, Columbus, Cincinnati and Indianapolis Railway Company to the Stockholders, for the Year Ending December 31st, 1885.* Short & Foreman, 1886.

Dacus, J.A. *Annals of the Great Strikes in the United States: A Reliable History and Graphic Descriptions of the Causes and Thrilling Events of the Labor Strikes and Riots of 1877.* L.T. Palmer & Co., 1877.

DeWitte, E.L. *Reports of Cases Argued and Determined in the Supreme Court of Ohio.* Robert Clark & Co., 1877.

Eastern Railway Company. *General Rules and Regulations of the Eastern Railroad Company, for the Government and Information of Employés* [sic] *Only: April 1878.* Rand, Avery & Co., 1878.

Enss, Chris. *Iron Women: The Ladies Who Helped Build the Railroad.* TwoDot, 2021.

Fernandez, Kathleen M. *Zoar: The Story of an Intentional Community*. Kent State University Press, 2019.

Foner, Philip S. *The Great Labor Uprising of 1877.* Monad Press, 1977.

Fortescue, William. "Paris Commune." In *Europe 1789–1914: Encyclopedia of the Age of Industry and Empire.* Vol. 4. Charles Scribner's Sons, 2006.

Garraty, John Arthur, and Mark C. Carnes, eds. *American National Biography.* Oxford University Press, 1999.

Hansen, Helen M. *At Home in Early Sandusky.* 1975.

Heywood, H.E. *The Great Strike: Its Relations to Labor, Property, and Government…* Co-operative Publishing Co., 1878.

Hoogenboom, Ari. *Rutherford B. Hayes: Warrior and President.* University Press of Kansas, 1995.

Huber, William R. *George Westinghouse: Powering the World*. McFarland & Company, 2022.

Jacobs, Timothy, ed. *The History of the Baltimore & Ohio: America's First Railroad.* Brompton Books, 1994.

———. *The History of the Pennsylvania Railroad.* Bison Books, 1988.

Joint Discussions Between Gen. Thomas Ewing of Ohio, and Gov. Stewart L. Woodford of New York, on the Finance Question; Held at Circleville, Wilmington, Tiffin, and Columbus, Ohio, October 2, 4, 8, and 9, 1875. 1876.

Journalist. *History of the Terrible Financial Panic of 1873: Graphic and Authentic Account of the Event; Downfall of the Money Kings…* 1873.

Jular, Clement. *A Brief History of Panics and Their Periodical Occurrence in the United States.* G.P. Putman's Sons, 1893.

Light, Walter. *Working for the Railroad: The Organization of Work in the Nineteenth Century.* Princeton University Press, 1983.

National City Company. *The Baltimore & Ohio Railroad Company: A Brief History of the Company Since It Began Service as a Common Carrier in 1827 Showing Its Development in Almost a Century of Service to the Public.* National City Company, 1924.

Nordhoff, Charles. *The Communistic Societies of the United States; from Personal Visit and Observation: Including Detailed Accounts of the Economists, Zoarites, Shakers, the Amana, Oneida, Bethel, Auroa, Icarian, and Other Existing Societies, Their Religious Creeds, Social Practices, Numbers, Industries, and Present Condition.* John Murray, 1875.

Oberholtzer, Ellis Paxson. *Jay Cooke: Financier of the Civil War*. Vols. 1 and 2. George W. Jacobs & Co., 1907.

Pinkerton, Allan. *Strikers, Communists, Tramps and Detectives.* G.W. Carleton & Co., 1878.

Pinpare, Stephen. *A People's History of Poverty in America.* New Press, 2008.

Reid, Whitelaw. *Ohio in the War: Her Statesmen, and Generals, and Soldiers.* Vol. 2. Moore, Wilstach & Baldwin, 1868.

Runswick, Brent. *Almost Worthy: The Poor, Paupers, and the Science of Charity in America, 1877–1917.* Indiana University Press, 2013.

Sander, Kathleen Waters. *John W. Garrett and the Baltimore & Ohio Railroad.* Johns Hopkins University Press, 2017.

Sipes, William B. *The Pennsylvania Road: Its Origin, Construction, Condition, and Connections…* Passenger Department, 1875.

Society of the Army of the Cumberland. *Society of the Army of the Cumberland, Nineteenth Reunion, Chicago, Illinois*. Robert Clark & Co., 1889.

Stowell, David O. *Streets, Railroads, and the Great Strike of 1877.* University of Chicago Press, 1994.

Tarbell, Ida. *The History of the Standard Oil Company*. Belt Publishing, 2018.

Vare, Ethlie Anne, and Greg Ptacek. *Patently Female: From AZT to TV Dinners, Stories of Women Inventors and Their Breakthrough Ideas.* John Wiley & Sons, 2002.

Vernon, Edward, ed. *American Railroad Manual for the United States and the Domain…* American Railroad Manual Company, 1874.

Wilson, William Bender. *History of the Pennsylvania Railroad with Plan of Organization, Portrait of Officials and Biographical Sketches.* Vol. 1. Henry T. Coates & Company, 1895.

Government Documents

Commonwealth of Pennsylvania. *Report of the Committee Appointed to Investigate the Railroad Riots in July, 1877.* Lane S. Hart, State Printer, 1878.

Hagan, F.M., comp. *Ordinances of the City of Springfield of a General and Permanent Nature in Force, October 1, 1880.* Transcript Printing Company, 1880.

Laurie, Clayton D., and Ronald H. Cole. *The Role of Federal Military Forces in Domestic Disorders, 1877–1945.* Center for Military History, United States Army, 1997.

Nimmo, Joseph, Jr., and United States. House of Representatives. 44th Congress. *First Annual Report on the Internal Commerce of the United States…* Government Printing Office, 1877.

Richardson, William A. *Annual Report on the State of Finances to the Forty-Third Congress, First Session, December 1, 1873.* Government Printing Office, 1873.

Ross, Philip W., and the United States Forest Service Eastern Region. *Allegheny Oil: The Historic Petroleum Industry on the Allegheny National Forest.* USDA Forest Service, Eastern Region, 1996.

State of Ohio. *Annual Reports for 1877: Made to the Sixty-Third General Assembly of the State of Ohio at the Regular Secession, Commencing January 7, 1878.* Part 2. Nevins & Myers, 1878.

United States. House of Representatives. Select Committee. 46th Congress, 2nd Session. *Causes of General Depression in Labor and Business; and as to Chinese Immigration.* Government Printing Office, 1879.

United States Army. Adjutant General's Office. *Index of General Court-Martial Orders, 1881.* Government Printing Office, 1882.

Wright, George B., and the State of Ohio. *Annual Report of the Commissioner of Railroad and Telegraphs to the Governor of the State of Ohio with Tabulations and Deductions from the Reports of the Railroad Corporations of the State for the Year Ending June 30, 1868.* Columbus Printing Company, State Printers, 1868.

Journals

Barreyre, Nicolas. "The Politics of Economic Crises: The Panic of 1873, the End of Reconstruction, and the Realignment of American Politics." *Journal of the Gilded Age and Progressive Era* 10, no. 4 (October 2011): 403–23.

Bernstein, Samuel. "American Labor in the Long Depression, 1873–1878." *Science & Society* 20, no. 1 (Winter 1956): 59–83.

Blatz, Perry K. "Pittsburgh: The Fiery Scape Goat for the County." *Western Pennsylvania History* 94, No. 3 (Fall 2011): 46–61.

Crombie, Helen. "Account of the Pennsylvania Railroad Riots from a Young Girl's Diary." Edited by John Newell Crombie. *Western Pennsylvania History* 5 (October 1971): 385–90.

Davis, William Z. "William H. West." *Ohio History Journal* 20, no. 4 (October 1911): 404–14.

Linn, Brian M. "Pretty Scaly Times: The Ohio National Guard and the Railroad Strike of 1877." *Ohio History Journal* 95 (August 1985): 171–81.

Lubetkin, M. John. "'No Fighting Is to Be Apprehended': Major Eugene Baker, Sitting Bull, the Northern Pacific Railroad's 1872 Western Yellowstone Surveying Expedition." *Magazine of Western History* 56, no. 2 (Summer 2006): 28–41.

Montague, Gilbert Holland. "The Rise and Supremacy of the Standard Oil Company." *Quarterly Journal of Economics* 16, no. 2 (February 1902): 265–92.

Munden, Christopher P. "Jay Cooke: Banks, Railroads, and the Panic of 1873." *Pennsylvania Legacies* 11, no. 1 (May 2011): 3–5.

Rice, Walter P., C.H. Burgess, and Hosea Paul, "Charles Paine." *Journal of the Association of Engineering Societies* 36, no. 5 (November 1906): 149–50.

Swartz, William. "The Wabash Railroad." *Railroad History* 133 (Fall 1975): 5–30

Taylor, Jan. "Marketing the Northwest: The Northern Pacific Railroad's Last Spike Excursion." *Montana: The Magazine of Western History* 60, no. 4 (Winter 2010): 16–35, 93–94.

Ullmo, Sylvia. "The Great Strikes of 1877." *Revue française d'études américaines*, no. 2 (October 1976): 49–56.

Magazines

Atlantic

Christian Union

Economist

Fire Lands Pioneer

Frank Leslie's Popular Monthly

International Review

Military History
Moody's Magazine
Nation, The
National Guardsmen—Supplement
New England Magazine
North American Review
Railroad Gazette
Railway News and Joint Stock Journal
Railway World

Newspapers

Belmont Chronicle (St. Clairsville, OH)
Centre Reporter (Centre Hall, PA)
Chicago Daily Tribune (IL)
Cincinnati Commercial (OH)
Cincinnati Enquirer (OH)
Cleveland Plain Dealer (OH)
Crestline Advocate (OH)
Daily Ohio State Journal (Columbus, OH)
Daily Ohio Statesman (Columbus, OH)
Daily Star (Cincinnati, OH)
Fremont Weekly Journal (OH)
Highland Weekly News (Hillsboro, OH)
Mansfield Herald (OH)
Massillon Daily Independent (OH)
Newark Advocate (OH)
New North-west (Deer Lodge, MT)
New York Herald (NY)
New York Times (NY)
Northern Ohio Journal (Painesville, OH)
Ohio Liberal (Mansfield, OH)
Perrysburg Journal (OH)
Pittsburgh Post (PA)
Stark County Democrat (OH)
St. Louis Globe-Democrat (MO)
Tiffin Tribune (OH)
Times (New Bloomfield, PA)
Workingman's Advocate (Chicago)

Online

American Social History Project/Center for Media and Learning. *1877: The Grand Army of Starvation Viewer's Guide*. SHEC: Resources for Teachers. shec.ashp.cuny.edu/items/show/1472.

Case Western Reserve. *Encyclopedia of Cleveland History*. case.edu/ech/articles/a/andrews-samuel.

National Governors Association. "Gov. Thomas L. Young." www.nga.org/governor/thomas-l-young.

"Railroad Costs Villages Money and Lives." bigwalnuthistory.org/Local_History/railroad/RR-Bad.htm.

INDEX

A

abolitionists 101
Adams Express Company 72
Allegheny Arsenal 72, 74
Allegheny City 67, 70, 75
Allegheny County 70
Allegheny County Workhouse 72
Allegheny River 72
Allegheny Valley Railroad 72
Allen, Milton 30
Allen, Tom 29
Alton Station 87
Altoona 69
Ammon, Robert 67, 68, 69, 70, 74, 75
Andrews, A.W. 41
Andrews, Clark & Company 59
Andrews, Samuel 59, 60, 80
Annual Report of the Commissioner of Railroad and Telegraphs 42
Antietam 14, 58
Ashby, Charles 89
Ashtabula County 45
Ashtabula River 44
Atlantic & Great Western Railway 42, 82
Atlantic, The 63
Auglaize County 79

B

Baggaley, Ralph 40
Baker, Eugene Mortimer 14, 16
Baltimore 48, 49, 50, 55, 99
Baltimore Boxes and Sawyer's Union 50
Baltimore & Ohio Railroad 8, 47, 48, 49, 50, 57, 61, 85, 89, 93, 96, 98, 99, 108
Belgium 104
Bellefontaine 106
Bellevue 44, 59
Bell, J.D. 101
Bergeret, Jules 104
Berkeley House 50

Berkeley Light Infantry 51
Bighorn River 17
Big Walnut Creek 45
Bimeler (Bäumler), Joseph Michael 31
Bishop, Richard M. 106
Black Hussars 71
Blandy, Henry 85
Blodgett, Amasa 32
Bloomingville 10
Board of Trade 84
Bohemia 79
Bonaparte, Louis Napoléon 103
Bonaparte, Napoléon 103, 104
Boody, Azariah 20
Boody House 84
Booth, Edwin 87
Boston 38, 82
Boston & Providence Railroad 38
Bozeman 15
Bradford oil field 63
Brannon, Mr. 43, 44
Brevoort Hotel 47
Brinton, Robert M. 70
Brooklyn Trust Company 16
Brown, Frank 96
Brown, George 48
Buffalo 29, 77, 98
Butler, Benjamin 90

C

California 91
Camden Station 49
Canada 59, 84, 108
Canadian Southern Railway 17
Capital University 67
Card, W.W. 40
Caroll, Matt 16
Carr, Charles W. 96, 97
Carver, William 44
Catholic Organ 91
Central Ohio Railroad 42, 48, 49
Central Vermont Railroad 79
Chambers, Arthur 29
Champion City Guard 97
Chapman Guards 79
charities 8, 26, 27
Chattanooga 58
Chicago 24, 25, 30, 68
China 68
cholera 83
Christian Union 102
Cincinnati 42, 49, 55, 89, 91, 93, 97, 107
Cincinnati Commercial 91
Cincinnati Enquirer 106
Cincinnati, Hamilton & Dayton Railroad 90, 91, 107
Cincinnati Home Guard 91
Cincinnati Law College 93
Cincinnati & Springfield Railway 81
Circleville 96
Civil War 8, 11, 14, 25, 30, 70, 82, 91, 101, 106
Clapp, Lizzie 38
Clark, Enoch W. 11
Clark, Maurice B. 59
Clements, William N. 55
Cleveland 28, 59, 60, 62, 77, 78, 79, 80, 81, 82, 83, 101, 104, 106
Cleveland, Cincinnati, Chicago & St. Louis Railroad 72
Cleveland, Columbus, Cincinnati & Indianapolis Railroad 81, 82
Cleveland Gatling Gun Battery 101
Cleveland, Mount Vernon & Columbus Railroad 45

Cleveland & Pittsburgh Railroad 77, 82
Cleveland Plain Dealer 79, 80
Cleveland Rolling Mill 81
Cleves 42
Coburn, Joe 29
Cogley, Elizabeth 37
Coinage Act 25
Coit, Mr. 29
Cold Creek 10
Collinwood 68, 78, 79
Colton 41
Columbia 58
Columbia Grammar School 77
Columbus 29, 67, 74, 85, 87, 93, 96, 97
Columbus, Piqua & Indianapolis Railroad 87
Communards 104
communism 7, 32, 82, 102, 104
"Communist and the Railway, The" 102
Communist Societies of the United States, The 31
Conference of Charities 27
Continental Bank 17
convict labor 25
Cooke, Eleutheros 10
Cooke, Jay 9, 10, 11, 14, 18
Cooke, Martha Caswell 10
Cooke, Pitt 10
Cooke's Castle 11, 20
Cooper, Peter 48
coopers' strike 79, 80, 81
cowcatcher 7, 43
Crestline 87
Crocker well 63
Crombie, Helen 71
Cross Creek 40
crude oil 59, 63
CSX 57
Custer, George 17

D

Darwin, Charles 27
Dayton 97
Dayton & Cincinnati Short Line 91
Decatur & East St. Louis Railway 20
Delaplaine, R.L. 51
Dělnické Listy (Workingmen's Journal) 79
Democratic Party 25
Dennison 96, 98
depression of the 1870s 7, 8, 9, 10, 18, 21, 23, 30, 32, 35, 47, 79, 91, 102
Derry 69
Devereux, John H. 81, 82
Diamond Hall 87
Dietrich's Hall 67
District of Columbia. *See* Washington, D.C.
doubleheader 45, 67, 69, 70, 99
double-track system 40
Drake, Charles 10
Dresden 83
Drew, Daniel 17, 20
Dugan, James 40, 41
Duluth 11, 14
Duncansville 58

E

Eastern Railway Company 38
East Liberty Stockyards 69
Eckert, Thomas T. 58

Economy 31
Edison, Thomas 38
Elkins Act 108
Ellicott's Mills 48
Elliott, Mr. 29
Ellis, John W. 20
Elyria 43, 44
Empire Transportation Company 63
Employees Relief Fund 108
England 48
Erie Canal 57
Erie Railroad 47, 63
Evolution 101
E.W. Clark & Company 11
Ewing, Thomas, Jr. 25

F

Fagaley, Mr. 89
Fahnestock, Harris C. 14, 17
Falley, Frederic 10
Faulkner, C.J. 51
Fenians 84
Fife, Richard H. 70, 71, 72
Fire Lands Pioneer 28
First Division of Philadelphia 70, 71, 72
First Troop of Light Cavalry (Troop A) 101
Fisk & Hatch 17
Fisk, James 17
Flagler, Henry M. 59, 60, 61, 62
Foner, Philip S. 50
Fort Churchill 14
Fort Ellis 15
Fort Loudon 58
Fort McHenry 54
Fort Sully 14
Foster Oil Company 63
France 61, 102, 103
Frank, Mr. 96
Fremont 43
Frémont, John C. 91
Fremont Weekly Journal 44
French, William H. 55

G

Gandy, Sheppard 16
Garrett, John W. 47, 49, 51, 78, 108
Germany 32, 33
Gesner, Abraham 59
Gettysburg 14
Gibbon, Catherine 38
Gibraltar Island 18
Ginn, Mr. 44
gold standard 25
Goodale Park 85
Gorman, Jack 15
Gould, Jay 17
Government of National Defense 103
Graham, Charles 40, 41
Graham, Frank D. 41
Grand Trunk Railroad 108
Grant Tunnel 40
Grant, Ulysses S. 9, 18
Granville 10
Grays 78
Great Labor Uprising of 1877, The 50
Great Lakes 20, 49, 63
greenbacks 23
Greenfield 28
Green Hill Cemetery 51
Grosvenor, Daniel 97

H

Haga, Godfrey 31
Hale, Edward E. 27
Halleck, Henry 91
Halpin, Jerry 42
Hampden-Sydney College 106
Hancock, Winfield Scott 54
Harmony Society 31
Harrisburg 58, 107
Hartranft, John F. 70, 74, 75
Havens, H.E. 41
Haydon, John A. 14, 15, 16
Hayes, Rutherford B. 8, 51, 74, 93
Heitmann, John H. 85
Hewitt, Issac L. 59
Holden, Maurice 97
Hooker, Joseph 58
Hopewell 59
Hotel de Ville 104
Hunt, Charles B. 98
Hunter's Point 80
Hutchinson's Battery 71, 72

I

Illinois 20
Indiana 10, 20
Indianapolis & Bellefontaine Railroad 81
insider trading 11
International Review 102
Interstate Commerce Commission 108
Ireland 84, 91

J

Jacob, Charles 89
Jay Cooke & Co. 9, 11, 17, 18
Jefferson College 106
Jewett, Hugh J. 47, 108
Johnson, Andrew 25
Johnson, Harvey 72
Johnson's Island 14
Johnston, W. 41
Jones, William W. 83, 84

K

Kansas 25
Kansas Free State Party 25
Kentucky 58, 106
kerosene 59, 61
Keynon, Cox & Company 16
Keyser, William 108
Killyleagh County 91
King, John, Jr. 50
knuckle-coupler 42

L

Lake Erie 10, 11, 20, 59, 63, 77
Lake Shore & Southern Michigan Railroad 9, 77, 78, 79, 81, 82
Lancaster 25
Laughlin, Thomas 29
Layng, J.D. 68
Leavenworth 25
Lewistown 58
Licking County 96
Lima 29
Lincoln, Abraham 37, 93

Little Miami Railroad 85
Locust Point 55
Loughery, David 96
Louis Philippe, King 103
Louisville 58
Louvre 104
Lutheran Church 31
Lynn, Albert 96

M

Madison 10
Mansfield 98
Mansfield Herald 98
Marietta & Cincinnati Railroad 28, 29, 49, 90, 91
Market Space 84
Martinsburg 50, 51, 55, 68
Maryland 57
Maryland legislature 48
Mason, James 29
Mathews, Henry M. 50, 51
Mathews Light Guard 51
Maumee Bay 84
McCrary, George W. 54
McDonald's Oil Factory 89
McLogan, P.H. 31
McMillan, John 89
McNeal, James 42
Mechanics' Banking Association 17
Metropolitan Hotel 108
Metropolitan National Bank 20
Michigan 17, 28
Michigan Central Railroad 78
Middle Grounds 83, 84
Milford Center 29
Military Division of the Atlantic 54
Mill Creek 89
Millsboro 106
Mingo Junction 40, 41
Mississippi River 20
Mississippi Valley 20
Missouri 41
Missouri–Kansas–Texas Railroad 16
Mitchell's Woods 28
Moest, William 41
Montana Territory 15
Moore, Albert 84
Moorehead, Sarah Cooke 10
Moorehead, William G. 10, 11
Moore, Robert M. 91
Moreau, George L. 41
Morris, Red 89
Moses Black's Dry Goods Store 98
Mount Vernon 96, 97
Mullaney, John "Buck" 89, 107
Murfey, Eliza 38

N

Nashville 58
National Bureau of Industry 106
National Guard (of Paris) 103, 104
National Trust Company 17
Nation, The 9
Neubert, Henry G. 84
Nevada 14
Newark 85, 93, 96, 97, 98
Newark Advocate 85, 96
Newark City Council 96
New Deal 26
New Hampshire 78
New Jersey 67
New Straitsville 97
New Vienna 29

New York Central Railroad 47, 57, 61, 63, 66, 77, 78, 108
New York (city) 9, 16, 17, 38, 47, 59, 62, 80, 91, 98, 108
New York & Harlem Railroad 9
New York Herald 104
New York (state) 10, 25, 27, 29, 31, 57, 59, 63, 83
New York Stock Exchange 18
New York Times 28
New York Tribune 17
Ninth Street Police Station 89
Nordhoff, Charles 31, 32
Norfolk Southern 57
North American Review 42
Northern Pacific Railway 11, 14, 16, 17, 20

O

Ogontz (chief) 10
Ogontz (Jay Cooke's Philadelphia estate) 11, 20
Ogontz Place. *See* Sandusky
Ohio 8, 10, 17, 20, 23, 25, 28, 30, 31, 40, 41, 42, 43, 44, 45, 49, 50, 59, 67, 68, 74, 79, 81, 83, 84, 89, 91, 93, 96, 98, 99, 104, 106, 107
Ohio & Erie Canal 32
Ohio House of Representatives 93
Ohio legislature 29, 106
Ohio & Mississippi Railroad 49, 89, 91, 107
Ohio National Guard 84, 87, 96, 97
Ohio River 48, 49, 57
Ohio Senate 93
118th Ohio Infantry 93
Oneida 31

P

Paine, Charles 78
Painesville 81
Palace of Versailles 104
Palda, Lev Jan 79, 80
Panhandle Railroad 40, 72, 85, 93
Panic of 1837 10
Panic of 1873 7, 8, 21, 60, 77
Paris 103
Paris Commune 103, 104
Parker 70
Parker, Oliver 90
Parkersburg 48, 49
Parma 59
Patterson, William 89
Patton, James 58
Pearson, Alfred L. 71, 75
Pennock, Charles 42
Pennsylvania 8, 31, 40, 57, 58, 59, 61, 63, 67, 70, 74, 106
Pennsylvania legislature 57, 61, 62
Pennsylvania Railroad (Pennsy) 8, 35, 37, 40, 45, 50, 57, 58, 59, 61, 62, 63, 66, 67, 68, 69, 70, 72, 74, 77, 93, 99
Perfectionists 31
Perry County 25
Philadelphia 9, 11, 17, 18, 57, 58
Philadelphia & Erie Railroad. *See* Sunbury & Erie Railroad
Phoenix Hall 69
Piketon 79
Pinkerton, Allan 67, 68, 74, 75
Pittsburgh 11, 40, 57, 58, 62, 67, 68, 69, 70, 71, 74, 85, 98, 99, 102, 107
Pittsburgh, Columbus, Cincinnati & St. Louis Railroad. *See* Panhandle Railroad

Pittsburgh, Fort Wayne & Chicago Railroad 50, 68, 69, 70, 75
Poisal, John 51
Portland (Maine) 38
Portland (Ohio). *See* Sandusky
Potomac River 48
Potts, Joseph D. 63
poverty 26, 27, 103
Prince Edward 106
Prussia 67, 103
Puget Sound 11
Pullman Company 72

Q

Quakers 31
Queens 80

R

railroad bridges, collapsing of 7, 43, 44
Railroad Safety Act 42
Reading 99, 107
rebates 51, 62, 108
Reconstruction 25
red scare 102
Republic 59
Republican Party 104, 106, 107
Richardson, William Adams 18
Richford 59
Riggin, Mary Isabelle 38
Robert Garrett & Sons 49
Roberts, William Milnor 14
Rockefeller & Andrews 59
Rockefeller, John D. 59, 60, 61, 62, 63
Rogers, George 28
Roosevelt, Franklin D. 26
Ross, W.D. 75

S

"Safety in Railway Travel" 42
Saint Paul 31
Sandusky 10, 11, 14, 49
Sandusky Bay 10
Sandusky City. *See* Sandusky
Sandusky Register 28
Sandusky River 43
San Francisco 91
Saratoga Springs 27
Schofield, Samuel H. 96
scientific charity 27
Scioto Valley Railroad 79
Scott, Thomas Alexander 58, 59, 66, 74, 78, 108
scrip 23
Second Empire 103
Second French Republic 103
Sedamsville 42
Seymour and Bool's store 10
Shakers 31, 32
Sharpsburg Bridge 72
Shawnee mines 97
Sherman, Mr. 29
Shoemaker, Robert M. 107
Shutt, A.P. 50
silver, price of 25
Sioux 14, 16, 17
Sitting Bull 14
Sixth Division of Pittsburgh 71
Skiddy, Francis 16
Smith, Samuel 87, 97
Society of Separatists of Zoar 32, 33

South Dakota 14
South Improvement Company 61, 62, 63
Southworth, Alvan S. 104
Spohn, Milton 85
Spotted Eagle 14
Springfield (Missouri) 41
Springfield (Ohio) 30, 96
Springton Forge 63
Standard Oil 59, 60, 61, 62, 63, 66, 79, 80, 81
Stanley, David Sloan 14
State Works System 57, 58
Steel, Alden 97, 98
Steubenville 40
St. Louis 10
St. Louis Globe-Democrat 72
Storing, William 40
"Story of a Great Monopoly, The" 63
Streeter, D.R. 30
strike-breakers 50
Strikers, Communists, Tramps and Detectives 74
Strongsville 59
Sullivan, Dennis 42
Sullivan, William 42
Sunbury 45
Sunbury & Erie Railroad 63
Sydney 91
Sykes, Hamlet 42

T

Tacoma 11
Tate, Daniel 40
Taylor, Zachary 25
Tennessee 82
Tennessee & Alabama Railroad 82
Thiers, Adolphe 104
Third Republic 103
Thomas, Philip E. 48
Thomson, John Edgar 58
Toledo 20, 78, 82, 83, 84, 87
Toledo & Cleveland Railroad 43
Toledo, Wabash & Western Railway (Toledo & Wabash Railroad) 17, 20, 41, 108
Tom Thumb 48
Townsend & Burgess Street Railway 85
train crew 8, 38, 47, 50
Trainmen's Union 50, 67, 68, 69, 70, 75
train, stopping time of 39
tramp 8, 23, 25, 27, 28, 29, 30, 31, 85, 90, 91
tuberculosis 38
Tuileries Palace 104
Turney, James 84
Tuscarawas County 31, 32
Tuttle, Henry B. 59
Tyler, Henry 108

U

Union army 25, 58, 91
Union Depot 85
Union Hotel 72
Union Station 72
Union Trust Company 17
United Kingdom 84
United States 7, 8, 21, 25, 28, 48, 51, 57, 59, 63, 68, 91, 102
University of Buffalo 83
U.S. Army 8, 14, 68, 91, 101
U.S. Congress 11, 30, 104, 108

U.S. Mint 25
Utah 20

V

vagrancy 30
  laws against 8, 30
Vallandigham, Clemet L. 25
Vanderbilt, Cornelius 77
Vanderbilt, William H. 47, 77, 79, 108
Vandergriff, William 51
Vendôme Column 104
Venice 10
Vose, George L. 42

W

Wabash Railway 20
Wabash & Western Railway 20
wage cuts 67, 81
Wall Street 16, 108
Walton, Mary 38
Wapakoneta 79
Warehouse & Security Company 16, 18
Washburne, Elihu Benjamin 104
Washington Arsenal 54
Washington, D.C. 17, 41
Washington Packet Line 11
Western Union 9, 58
Westinghouse airbrake 39, 40
Westinghouse, George 39, 40
West Point 14
West Virginia 8, 48, 50, 68
West, William H. 106
Whalan, William 90
Wheeling 48, 49, 51
Wheeling & Lake Erie Railroad 32
Wilson, Frank 29
Windsor Hotel 108
Woodford, Stewart L. 25
Wood, Ira 90
Workingman's Advocate 30
Württemberg 31

Y

Yellowstone River 15
Yellowstone Valley 14, 17
York 48
Young, Thomas L. 91, 93, 96, 97, 98, 99

Z

Zanesville 85, 87, 96, 97
Zepp, Dick 55
Zepp, George 55
Zoar Hotel 32
Zoar Village 31, 32

ABOUT THE AUTHOR

Award-winning author Mark Strecker has wanted to be a writer since he first learned to read. He graduated from Bowling Green State University with a bachelor of arts degree in history in 1994 and a master's degree in library science from Clarion University in 2008, earning the latter to give him the skills needed to write well-researched narrative history. A lifelong resident of Ohio, his greatest passions are history (no surprise there), travel, reading, and comic book collecting. On his website, www.markstrecker.com, in addition to articles, he posts travel logs about the various historic sites and museums he's visited, most of which are in the Buckeye State.

Visit us at
www.historypress.com